Clockwise

intermediate

Classbook

Will Forsyth

OXFORD

UNIVERSITY PRESS

Contents

01
ALL IN THE MIND

In this Unit
- Practise starting conversations.
- Look at different question forms.
- Learn to record new words in sentences.

Speaking
Know your mind

1 Find out the name of everyone in the group. Pronounce it correctly.
  1 Think of four things you'd like other people to know about you. Tell the group.
  2 Change groups. Talk about people in the first group.

2 In pairs, do the Mind Quiz. Keep to the time limits. Compare your results in each section, 1 to 10.

Find your personal learning style with …

THE MIND QUIZ

1 Occasions   seconds

Think of an occasion when you got a number of presents, e.g. your birthday. What presents did you get? Who gave them to you?

2 People   seconds

Think of ten people you've talked to in the last seven days.

Improve your memory

Get to know your learning style.

- All ten types of memory in the Quiz are useful for learning language. Try using the ones you are good at. Practise the ones you are not so good at.
- Each Unit in the course contains a learning technique. Use them to learn English faster and remember it longer.

3 Words   seconds

a What did Neil Armstrong say when he stepped onto the moon?
b How many words can you think of for describing people?

4 Music   seconds

a Sing, whistle, or hum a tune you know.
b What tunes go with these words?
'I'm singin' in the rain, just singin' in the rain.'
'But more, much more than this, I did it my way.'

5 Numbers   seconds

How many telephone numbers can you remember? Whose are they?

6 Concepts   seconds

a What's the difference between these words: *know*, *think*, *remember*, *forget*, *recall*, *learn*, *memorize*?
b What is an 'auxiliary verb'?

7 Spaces and places   seconds

What's your favourite place like, indoors or outdoors? Describe it.

8 Feelings   seconds

How does it feel to be very happy? Describe the feeling.

9 Future arrangements   seconds

What plans have you got? Say the day, date, time, and place of three arrangements you have.

10 Recent events   seconds

What presents did your partner say he/she got in Question 1? How many presents can you remember? Who gave them?

3 Identify your strengths.
  1 Which three types of memory did you find easiest?
  2 Does your partner agree? How similar are you?

Question types

1 Look at two different types of question.

Questions with *be*
a **Are you** from South America?
b **What are** your plans for this evening?

Object questions
c What sort of things **do you enjoy** doing?
d **Did you do** anything interesting at the weekend?

1 Find more examples in the Mind Quiz.
2 How do we make questions with *be*?
3 Make a list of the auxiliaries we can use to make object questions.
4 Why are they called 'object' questions?

2 In groups, find out about your teacher.

1 Write as many questions of each type as you can.
2 Take turns to ask your questions. Don't repeat questions from other groups.

3 Look at the pattern of these questions.

Subject questions
e **Who** wants to go out this evening?
f **How many people** want to come?

1 Find two more examples of this type in the Mind Quiz.
2 Divide them into two parts.
Who wants / to go out this evening?
3 How are they different from object questions?

4 Look at these examples of reporting questions.

Reporting questions
g Do you know where the restaurant is?
h What time do you think we should meet?

1 Find another example in the Mind Quiz.
2 Divide them into two parts. Underline the question forms.
3 Correct these reporting questions.
  1 Why you think we forget things?
  2 You know how we remember things?
  3 You can remember what you learned in your first English lesson?
  4 What methods you think most people use to remember things?

5 [○1] Listen to example questions **a** to **h**.
1 Underline the stressed words.
2 Listen again and repeat. Copy the intonation.

 Against the clock!

6 Set a time limit
In pairs, make complete questions.

Learning English	How do you do it?

1 (why / you / decide) to learn English?
Why did you decide to learn English?
2 (what / your best) subject at school?
3 (you / think) (you / better at) learning now than you were ten years ago?
4 (what / your most successful) learning experience?
5 (how / you learn) new words?
6 (rules / help) you learn to use a language? How?
7 (what / 'learn' / mean)?
8 (what / make) learning fun?
9 (you / think) (you / remember) things better when you're having fun?
10 (what / make) people successful learners?

7 Now relax. Change partners. Ask and answer the questions.

Questions with *be*
  What's your name?
  Are you good at learning languages?
To make a question with *be*, we invert (↶↷) the subject and verb.

Object questions
  What does Jill study at college? (Jill studies) **economics**.
  Did you see **Sergio** yesterday? No, I didn't (see **him**).
These questions ask about the object of a sentence (*economics / Sergio*). They need an auxiliary, e.g. *am / are, does / did, have / has*, modals *can / will*, etc.

Subject questions
  Who told you? **Hiroshi** (told me).
  What happens after lunch? **Nothing** (happens).
These questions ask about the subject (*Hiroshi / Nothing*). They don't take an auxiliary. They nearly always begin with *who* or *what*. They are in the same order as the statement (subject / verb / object).

Reporting questions
  Where **do you think** he went?
  Do you agree that we should talk in English?
There are two verbs in reporting questions. Only the first one has a question form, e.g. *Do you think / agree ...?*

If you want to learn a language, get a dog

Reading
Get a dog

1 Match the words with their meanings.

1	awkward	*b*	**a**	talk to someone in a comfortable way
2	acquaintance	☐	**b**	uncomfortable
3	chat	☐	**c**	the money someone earns at work
4	cheerful	☐	**d**	someone you know a little
5	wages	☐	**e**	happy

2 Read the article. Explain the title.

When I arrived in Moscow, all my friends and colleagues gave different advice about the best way to learn Russian. It is easy to find a teacher: Russia is full of underpaid (or unpaid) academics who will explain every word and tense for a dollar or two. No one, however, suggested getting a dog but that is what we did. And Rupert, as he is called, has introduced me to a large number of acquaintances. I can now stand around chatting to local dog owners while our animals run and play.

It may not sound much, but it is a real achievement in a city where getting to talk to people is not easy. Russians are just as reserved as the British when it comes to meeting people. Like the British, they have forgotten what to do. Some shake hands. Some don't, they just say 'zdravstvuytye' ('hello') and most Russians will reply 'normalno' ('all right'), which is not exactly cheerful. And there the conversation usually ends.

Not so with the dog owners. 'Look at that,' Andrei, a complete stranger, said to me without a moment's awkwardness; he was looking at his dog. 'He brought back 24 ducks last year. That's what I call a good hunting dog.' And before long, we were deep in conversation about his shockingly low and delayed wages, politics, and books; and all without one 'normalno' or awkward handshake to make us feel uncomfortable.

The Independent

3 What does the article say about …?
1 finding a language teacher
2 meeting people
3 what to do and say when you meet people
4 what acquaintances talk about

4 Tell a partner two ways to meet foreigners in your country.

Vocabulary
Word groups

1 Add these words to the correct word group.

acquaintance	colleague	suggest
reserved	chat	say
reply	cheerful	stranger
teacher	dog owner	uncomfortable

Word group	Examples
People	*friends …*
'Talking' verbs	*explain …*
Feelings	*awkward …*

2 In pairs, how many more words can you add in two minutes?

3 Mark the stress on the words in ex.1.

acquaintance

4 Complete the story with the words / endings on the left.

me
that
them
to
for
-ing

1 I was talking / a colleague one day   *I was talking to a colleague one day …*
2 and I explained / I wanted / learn English
3 she suggested find / an English conversation group
4 and she introduced / an American woman
5 we went / a café and chatted / some people in English / an hour
6 the atmosphere was informal and made / feel very comfortable
7 now I meet / every Saturday morning

Vocabulary tip

When you meet a new word:
- Make a note of it, e.g. *advice*.
- Underline the stressed syllable (ad<u>vice</u>).
- Make a note of how to use it:
  give advice
  (They gave me different advice.)
  advice + about (how to learn Russian)

Listening
Greetings

1 [●2] Listen to five conversations. Make notes like this for each one.

	1	2	3	4	5
• Where are they?					
• What's happening?					
• Formal/informal?					

2 Listen again. Tick the expressions you hear.

☐ Excuse me   ☐ How're things?   ☐ What've you been up to?
☐ Hello   ☐ Good to see you   ☐ How are you?
☐ Hi   ☐ Hi there
☐ Hiya   ☐ Pleased to meet you

3 Which expressions are the most formal? Which are the least formal?

English in use
Starting conversations

1 Look at these extracts from the five conversations.

   1 Look at the four questions in **bold**. Are they complete/incomplete?

> 1 A **Can you tell me where the International Department is, please?**
>   B On the first floor of C Block. ....
>
> 2 C Hello, hi
>   D Hiya, all right?
>   C **How're things?** ....
>
> 3 E Hear you been to Spain. ... How long for?
>   F Just for a week.
>   E Not long enough then, eh! ....

> 4 H Hi there.
>   G Hello, hi. Come in. Pleased to meet you.
>   I Hello there.
>   G First of all, **would you like a cup of tea or coffee?**
>   H Love one. Thought you'd never ask. ....
>
> 5 J Haven't seen you for ages. **What've you been up to?** ....

   2 Tick any incomplete sentences / questions.

2 [●3] Listen and copy the intonation.

3 Think of a different way of completing the 'starting phrases' in the box. Walk around the class. Start different conversations.

Speak out
Improvise

1 In pairs, choose one of the photos.

   Where are they?   Have they met before?   What are they talking about?

2 Make up their conversation. Don't write it down – just do it.

3 Now be yourself. Talk to one or two people.

   • Say hello and ask how they are. Find out what they've been up to.
   • Continue chatting, e.g. ask them if they'd like ... a cup of coffee/to meet later ...

Starting phrases

These four phrases are very useful for starting conversations.

> Can you tell me (where/what/ who/when ...)?
> How're things?
> I hear you ('ve been to Spain).
> What've you been up to?

Notice that we often use incomplete sentences/questions in speech.

Remember

• Use a variety of ways of starting conversations.

• Try to include different kinds of questions.

• Practise chatting to find out about your partner's recent activities.

02 CHANGING WORLD

In this Unit

- Practise being imprecise.
- Use present tenses to discuss change.
- Associate new words with places, to help you remember them.

Speaking
Change

1 What has changed in the last year? Write two changes for each circle.

you   your family   your country   the world

2 In pairs, compare your answers. How do you hope that these things will change over the next two to ten years?

Reading
Picking out important points

1 Turn to *p.99*. Find Taiwan and Afghanistan. Describe where they are (*near / next to / north of* ..., etc.). What do you know about them?

2 Quickly read about Taiwan.
   1 With a highlighter, mark what you understand. For the moment, ignore what you don't understand.
   2 Read again. Make notes about ...
     • the most surprising thing in the article
     • similarities between your country and Taiwan
     • differences between your country and Taiwan
     • how Taiwan is changing

TAIWAN – the difference

Asia is different, they say. But Taiwan, for example, has a successful, modern, capitalist economy. It is now the world's third largest exporter of high-tech goods like computers. It believes in doing business and making money. So how is it different?

One major difference, according to Professor Jessica Lu from the Psychology Department of Kaohsiung Medical School, is that here, in the West, we keep work and family life separate. But in Taiwan there is no difference. So, for example, they have the ground floor of a building as a shop or office, and the family lives on the second floor.

Also, in Taiwan, family businesses stay in the family. But as family firms get big, they need more people (i.e. sons) to run them. So where do all the sons come from? In the words of Professor Lu, 'from wives without a title': a rich man decides how many sons he will need to run his business, and then he finds a number of wives to provide them. And the wives all live in the same house, calling each other sisters. 'There is only one official wife, recognized by the law,' says Professor Lu, 'but the others don't mind.'

This is still true today, and there will be a conflict when more multi-national companies come into Taiwan to invest. And it is changing, but very very slowly, and these Taiwanese businesses will survive because they have survived for thousands of years.

In Business

   3 Compare your notes in pairs.

3 Look at words / expressions you didn't understand. Explain them to each other or use a dictionary.

4 Choose up to ten words / expressions to learn. Make a note of them.

FACT FILE AFGHANISTAN

POPULATION	22m
CAPITAL CITY	Kabul
RELIGION	1 _Islam_

GOVERNMENT

The Taliban Movement, since 2 _____ .
The Taliban dislikes Western influences.
It has:

- banned 3 _____ , _____ , and
  _____ .
- smashed and publicly hanged 4 _____ .
- burnt 5 _____ .
- but has allowed people to keep 6 _____
  and _____ as long as they weren't
  using them.

CURRENT SITUATION

- The changes do not have public support.
  Large numbers of people are still
  watching 7 _____ and _____ .
- Shop owners and private citizens have
  been ordered to throw out their 8 _____ ,
  _____ , and _____ within 15 days.

Vocabulary **tip**

Mentally, put new words and
phrases ...

- in places on a map (see _p.99_)
- in the place where you learned
  them
- in different places around your
  house.

When you want to remember a
word, remember where you put it.
This memory technique is at least
2,000 years old!

Listening
Afghanistan

1 In groups, read about
Afghanistan. Guess the
missing words.

2 [○ 1] Listen to a news
item about Afghanistan.
Complete the text.

3 Look at the words in
italics. Are they verbs
or nouns?

  1 How is Afghanistan
changing?

  2 What social _movement_ happened in Europe and North America in the 1960s?

  3 How does the USA _influence_ your country?

  4 Are there any _bans_ in your country that you disagree with?

4 Find a form of the _italic_ words from ex.3 in the Fact File. Which three
words can be used as either verbs or nouns?

5 Ask and answer the four questions from ex.3 in pairs.

6 Do these kinds of reports help us to understand other countries?

Vocabulary
Describing the world

1 Look at these 'world' words. How do you pronounce them?

Geography	People/Culture	Politics/Economics
an island	religious	a democracy
the mainland	traditional	capitalist
humid	modern	socialist
mountainous	conservative	to produce
open spaces	hard-working	to export
densely populated		a social security system

2 Match each word with one part of the world. Explain your match in
pairs.

3 What are the nationalities and languages of these countries?

Britain	Egypt	Japan	Poland	Thailand
China	France	Korea	Portugal	Turkey
Czech Republic	Germany	Mexico	Russia	
Denmark	Greece	Netherlands	Spain	

4 Pronounce them correctly. Use the table below.

-ish -an/-ian/-ican	-ese	other
Danish Egyptian	Japanese	French
These words are always stressed on the syllable before the -ish, -an, -ian, or -ican ending.	These words are always stressed on the -ese ending.	Most of these words are only one syllable.

The present

When you are talking about the present you can:
1 describe the status quo.
All life **needs** water.
The Earth **goes** round once every 24 hours.
2 describe changes to the status quo.
   a Changes happening now:
   The Earth **is getting** warmer.
   b Changes up to now:
   The Earth **has got** warmer in the last 100 years.

1 Do the Quiz in pairs. Circle **a**, **b**, or **c** each time.

THE TURNING WORLD QUIZ

1 The Earth goes round the sun once a ▓.
   a day   **b** month   **c** year
2 The moon goes round the Earth once every ▓ days.
   a 12   **b** 28   **c** 35
3 There are about ▓ independent countries in the world.
   a 75   **b** 200   **c** 400
4 People grow crops on ▓ of the Earth's land surface.
   a 1%   **b** 10%   **c** 50%
5 About ▓ of the world's population lives in cities.
   a 10%   **b** 40%   **c** 80%
6 The biggest continent is ▓ (43,608,000 sq kms).
   a Africa   **b** Asia   **c** S. America
7 The world spends about ▓ billion a year on 'defence'.
   a $25   **b** $300   **c** $800

   1 Check your answers on p.99.
   2 In pairs, say the answers. Remember the sentences.

2 Answer questions 1 to 8.

The Changing State of the Nation

Write True (**T**) or False (**F**) for your country.   T/F
1 *Life is getting better for most people.*   ☐
2 *Everything in my country is changing too fast.*   ☐
3 *We're forgetting our traditions.*   ☐
4 *Families are becoming less important.*   ☐

In your opinion …
5 *Has your country changed for the better in the last ten years?*
6 *Has marriage gone out of fashion?*
7 *Have people in the towns forgotten simple things – like where their food comes from?*
8 *Has life become less fun in the last ten years or so?*

   1 Which questions ask about changes happening now?
   2 Which questions ask about changes up to now?

3 Look at the True / False sentences (1 to 4) again. Make them all true for your country.
Life is getting better for a few people, and worse for most people.

 Against the clock!

4 Set a time limit ▓
In pairs, make sentences / questions.

how do you feel about CHANGE?

Are these sentences True (T) or False (F) for you personally?
                                                                        T/F
1 I (not change) *haven't changed* much since I was a child.   ☐
2 I can stop learning now because I (learn) _____ everything I need. ☐
3 My closest friends are people I (meet) _____ in the last two years. ☐
4 Sometimes I (not know) _____ where (life take) _____ me.   ☐
5 I (still look) _____ for the right job or career.   ☐
6 Things (usually happen) _____ to me by chance.   ☐
7 I (not usually enjoy) _____ change.   ☐
8 I (not look) _____ for change at the moment: I'm happy as I am. ☐

Answer these questions.
9 (you think) _____ of changing jobs in the near future?
10 (you stop) _____ changing?
11 (your interests be) _____ different now from two years ago?
12 (what improve) _____ in your life so far?
13 (there be) _____ something in the future that (you try) _____ to achieve in life?
14 (you think) _____ it's important for people to change?
15 (you decide) _____ what your next change is going to be?
16 (you currently wait) _____ for something to happen to you?

5 Now relax. Choose ten of the questions or T / F sentences. Interview someone.

6 Write an example for each tense in the chart. Translate the examples. What tense do you use in your language?

Present simple	Present continous	Present perfect
describing now	current changes	changes up to now
⊢┼┼┼┼┼⊣	∿↯∿	∿⏐
NOW	NOW	NOW

English in use
Being vague

1 True or false? Decide in pairs.

  1 The population of Hong Kong is six million.

  2 Hong Kong consists of two islands.

  3 Part of Hong Kong is on the mainland of China.

  4 Hong Kong is very densely populated – there are no open spaces.

  5 In summer, the temperature reaches 45 degrees and humidity can be 100%.

  6 There are 19,000 restaurants in Hong Kong.

  7 There is a social security system.

2 **02** Listen to Steve. Were you right?

3 Listen again.

  1 Notice the first four expressions from the **Vague expressions** box.

  2 Complete the 'Did you know?' text. Use each expression twice.

DID YOU KNOW... ?

1 There are *about* 200 independent countries in the world.

2 _____ Afghans watch satellite channels on TV.

3 _____ 50% of people in the world have never seen a telephone.

4 People in Iceland _____ have two jobs because life is so expensive.

5 Human beings are _____ 1 million years old.

6 There _____ be an ice age every 100 million years.

7 _____ earthquakes occur in a ring around the Pacific Ocean, called 'The Ring of Fire'.

8 Cities have _____ 10% less snow and 10% more cloud than the countryside.

4 Find expressions from the **Vague expressions** box which ...

  • describe a place by giving an example
  • introduce a new topic

5 **03** Listen. Which country do you think this is?

6 **04** Listen and copy the intonation.

7 Use the expressions. Say three things about your country.

  • something you are proud of

  • something you don't like very much

  • what you like best

Vague expressions

Steve uses these expressions when he doesn't want to be precise.

about
  ... the population of Hong Kong is, it's about six million

a large number of
  there are a large number of islands

tend to
  there tend to be, open spaces and then very densely populated areas

up to
  The humidity can be sometimes up to about 100%.

Steve also uses these expressions.

as far as ... is concerned
  As far as the climate's concerned, in the summer, it reaches 34°...

the sort of place where
  It's the sort of place where everybody has to be responsible for themselves financially.

Speak out
Talking about your country

1 What should people know about your country? What would you like to know about other countries, e.g. people, politics ...?

2 Choose a topic(s). In pairs, make notes about your country. Say ...

  • what it's like now
  • how it has changed

  • how it's changing
  • what you think of it

3 Take turns to talk about your country.

Remember

• Use present tenses to describe status quo and change.

• Include the vocabulary you've studied to describe people, politics, geography, etc.

• Try to use 'vague' phrases when you can't/don't want to be precise.

03
LIFE STORY

In this Unit

- Practise telling stories and using question tags.
- Talk about things that have happened with past simple / present perfect.
- Look at vocabulary for talking about life stages.

Vocabulary tip

Put words / phrases in a logical order.

- in the order they always happen (birth, childhood ..., etc.)
- in the order they've happened to you (went to college, met Frances ..., etc.)

The order needn't be 'correct' – it's only to help you remember.

Speaking and vocabulary
Stages of life

1 Find these life stages in the photos. Which is the best? Why?
   - a child
   - a married couple with young children
   - a young adult (17 – 30)
   - a middle-aged couple

2 Think about life events. In pairs, **A** turn to *p.99*, **B** to *p.103*.

3 Choose ten life events. Choose an order for them which means something to you. Then remember your lists in pairs.

Reading
Nomad

1 What qualities does someone need to become successful from nothing? Think of four.

2 Read about Waris Dirie. In pairs, decide on:
   1 the four most important events in her life
   2 three pieces of luck
   3 two examples of strength and determination

3 Tell a partner about someone you admire.

'Once I was worth 5 camels

... now I can earn £5,000 a day!'

The story of Waris Dirie

'When I was a girl, in the deserts of Somalia, my family was nomadic, moving around with our animals. We were happy, and I loved my mother more than anything.

I was about 13 when my father called me at the end of a hot day. 'Come and sit here,' he said. 'I've found you a husband! We have arranged that he will give me five camels.' That night I ran away. I was frightened. For almost three weeks, I walked through the desert, but finally I got to my auntie's house in Mogadishu. Auntie's husband was an ambassador and in a few months I flew to Britain to work at his London house.

One day, a photographer called Michael Goss saw me in the street. He took my picture and the photographs were beautiful. 'You should try and do modelling,' he told me. When my aunt and uncle returned to Africa, I stayed in London. I found a place to stay and got a job at McDonald's. Then one day I took Michael Goss's photographs to an agency. They sent me to a studio, and my picture appeared on the cover of the Pirelli calendar. Soon after that, the agency got me a part in the James Bond film *The Living Daylights*.

That was seven years ago. Since then I've done modelling all over the world and I've appeared in magazines such as *Vogue* and *Elle*. I have even hosted the US music programme *Soul Train*. Once, I was worth five camels. Now I can earn up to £5,000 for one day's work. I have gone from the bottom to the top.

TV Quick

The past simple and the present perfect

The story of the first woman doctor

a [1] Elizabeth Blackwell was the first woman doctor.

b [ ] but really, she wanted to be a doctor.

c [ ] but she qualified as a doctor **in** 1849.

d [ ] **After that**, she worked in Europe **for** a few years, **and then** went back to New York and opened an all-women hospital **in** 1857.

e [ ] She died in London **in** 1910 **when** she was 89.

f [ ] but she **finally** got a place at medical school. Her fellow students refused to talk to her,

g [ ] She was born in Bristol, England, **in** 1821 and the family lived there **until** she was 11, **but then** they moved to New York.

h [ ] The medical schools in New York City refused to take her because she was a woman,

i [ ] Her father died **when** she was 17, **so** she left school and became a teacher to support the family,

1 Read about Elizabeth Blackwell. Number the sentences in order.

1 What tense are all the verbs in? Do they describe finished periods or unfinished periods?

2 What 'jobs' do the linking words / phrases in **bold** do?

'After that' – *describes the order of events*

The 'closed' past

The past simple is the usual tense for talking about the past. We use it to describe events and periods which finished in the past.

I **left** school early because I hated it.   NOW

We **moved house** three times when I was young.

We **stayed** in Montreal for five years.

[five years]

We use it to say:

- **that** something happened, or was true.
  I had a dog once.
- **when** things happened.
  We got married five years ago / in 1996.
- **what order** things happened in.
  We got married and then moved here.

We use it to tell stories:

I walked for three weeks. Finally, I got to the city ...

---

2 Read the sentences. Who is it?

a He's been married twice and has five children.

b He's been to college and has a teaching qualification.

c He's worked as a primary school teacher.

d He's been unemployed.

e He's played with a band called The Police and he's been a solo artist for many years.

f He's written a lot of best-selling songs. They've made him a pop superstar.

g He's helped to raise money for 'The Rainforest Foundation' which works with Amazonian Indians.

3 Look at sentences **a** to **g** in ex.2 again.

1 What tense are the verbs in?

2 Do the sentences tell you ...?

- what he does now (schoolteacher, married, etc.)
- when he did these things

The 'collective' past

Think of the present perfect as a kind of net in which you collect past experiences. We use the present perfect:

- to talk about our collection of life-time experiences.
  *He's **had** three jobs and **been married** twice.*
- to describe the present result of past events.
  *His songs **have made** him a pop superstar.*

BUT NOT to say **when** events happened, OR **what order** they happened in, OR to **tell a story** about them.

 Against the clock!

4 Set a time limit

In pairs, choose the correct verb forms.

1 Waris Dirie's photograph **was / has been** on the Pirelli calendar in 1988.

2 Waris Dirie **was / has been** very lucky in her life.

3 Waris Dirie **worked / has worked** first as a model, then as an actress.

4 Sting **became / has been** a solo artist ever since he left The Police.

5 Sting **wrote / has written** 'Every Breath You Take' in half an hour one night.

6 The Rainforest Foundation **made / has made** more than £2 million in the period up to '93.

5 Now relax. Make six sentences about your parents.

- their childhood
- meeting / marriage
- the last few years
- work
- where they've lived
- their schooldays / education

They met when they were at school.
My dad's been a teacher and an engineer.
They've lived in Madrid since 1974.

Listening
Determination

1 Read the beginning of the story. What do you think it's about?

Rainforest man's long journey to Oxford

Indian goes from hunting monkeys in the jungle to studying politics at university.

Miguel Hilario left his simple village life in the Amazon jungle for the academic life as a student at Oxford.

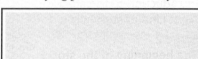

2 Listen to a radio interview with Miguel.

  1 Put these phrases in the order they happened.

- [ ] four or five days in a canoe to the closest city, Pucallpa
- [1] my dad trained me to survive in the jungle / fishing, hunting, canoeing
- [ ] I was on the street for two months / leftover food from the Chinese restaurant
- [ ] a Peruvian family gave me food in exchange for work
- [ ] a scholarship to study in Texas, then Oxford
- [ ] worked during the day / went to school at night / taught myself Spanish
- [ ] some missionaries offered me a place to stay and a job
- [ ] further education in Lima
- [ ] I studied theology and linguistics

  2 What kind of person do you think he is?

3 Listen again.

  1 What were Miguel's answers to these questions?

    1 What was your life like when you were growing up there?

    2 So how did you get to your first school, then, to get your education?

    3 You were taken in by a Peruvian family, there, weren't you?

    4 How did you live when you were in Lima?

    5 And you then got a scholarship to study in Texas, didn't you?

  2 Check your answers with the Tapescript on *p.106*.

4 What do you think of Miguel and Waris Dirie, and their lives so far?

  1 Compare them using these words / phrases.

Adjectives		Nouns	
They are ...		**They've needed ...**	**They've had ...**
de<u>ter</u>mined	am<u>bi</u>tious	determi<u>na</u>tion	good luck / bad luck
<u>si</u>milar	strong	strength	suc<u>cess</u>
different	suc<u>cess</u>ful	imagi<u>na</u>tion	
		am<u>bi</u>tion	

  2 What are the five essentials for success?

5 Imagine you made a big change in your life. Where would you go and what would you do?

English in use
Telling true stories in conversation

1 Match the events in Miguel's story to stages 1 to 5 in the box.

☐ — and he went to school, first of all in a rainforest town, and then to college in Lima, and then he went to study in the United States,

☐ — This is a heart-warming story of real determination.

☐ — which shows the remarkable lengths people will go to to avoid Sting!

☐ — It's about this young man from Peru, born in the rainforest, but he had a dream that he would be educated,

☐ — and then finally he's now ended up as a postgraduate student at Oxford University,

2 Listen to someone telling the story. Check your answers.

3 Underline some of the expressions from the box below in Miguel's story. Use them to quickly tell the true story of Waris Dirie, Sting, or someone else.

Expressions for telling true stories

Stage 1   **This is a** (funny / sad / terrible, etc.) story

Stage 2   **It's about** (my father / someone I met at college)

Stage 3   **First, and, (and) then, next, after that,** etc. (+ simple past)

Stage 4   **and so / finally / in the end** (he got what he wanted)
and so now (he's very happy / she's become very rich)

Stage 5   **which** (I think is awful / great)

4 Look back at the interviewer's questions to Miguel (**Listening** ex.3). Which questions did she already know the answers to?

5 Write the question tags for these questions.
1 You went to school in Rome, _____ ?
2 You were the second daughter, _____ ?
3 You were an only child, _____ ?
4 And then you went to university, _____ ?
5 You started playing volleyball when you were 16, _____ ?

6 Listen and check. Then repeat. Copy the intonation.

Speak out
Your life story

1 Make a diagram like this of your life so far.

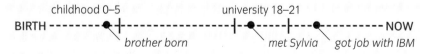

1 Divide it into four or five stages. Add approximate ages.
2 Add notes about the most important events, e.g. *university – met Sylvia*.

2 In pairs, swap diagrams and interview each other.

04
SOMETHING TO DO

In this Unit

- Practise getting information and active listening.
- Look at uses of the gerund (*-ing*) and infinitive (*to ...*).
- Talk about things you enjoy; make suggestions and respond.

Speaking
A good time

1 Can you remember two recent occasions which you really enjoyed?
2 Look at the photos. Describe what's happening.

A  B  C

Reading
Things to do

1 In groups, think of things to do in a free weekend ...
- with friends
- by yourself

2 Read the article. Write the numbers of the activities in each column.

Things I've done	Things I'd like to do	Things I wouldn't like to do

3 Has the article given you any other ideas? Make more suggestions in groups. Vote for the two best.

---

15 ways to enjoy the weekend

Next weekend, why not do something different? Here are some suggestions to get you going!

1 Go skiing Get some friends together and find a dry ski slope near you.

2 Kick a football around All you need is some space and a few friends.

3 Second-hand shops You might even find something valuable. Or try and sell some of your own old stuff!

4 Can't afford the Caribbean? Then give yourself a mini beach holiday – in the garden. Get yourself a long cold drink and spend the day with a best-seller from your favourite author. Heaven!

5 Go window shopping It's free!

6 Lazy entertaining Ask your friends round for dinner. Ask each one to bring a different course, so there's less work for you!

7 Surprise an old friend Telephone someone you haven't spoken to for ages and have a good long chat.

8 Be a tourist Go on a guided tour of your nearest city. You'll be surprised how much you never noticed before!

9 Make a splash Go down to the swimming pool and jump off the diving board.

10 Go flying Many companies these days can take you up in a two-seater plane or hot-air balloon, or glider. And most offer an introductory lesson at half price.

11 Discover history Wherever you live, your local tourist office will give you details of a castle, Stone Age camp, or ancient monument near you.

12 Have a picnic And if it rains, just have it on the floor at home!

13 Get away If you live in the city, rent a country cottage with some friends for the weekend, or go camping.

14 Learn something new It's never too late to take up a new interest: Flamenco dancing, African drumming, literature, or car mechanics.

15 Relax Rent a few of your favourite films on video. Make it into a real cinema event: buy some popcorn, turn the lights down low, and invite some friends round. □

Listening

A full life

dance music
running
hot-air ballooning
swimming
playing the guitar
drumming
going for drives in the car
jumping off diving boards

1 Magnus Collins is a musician and he's blind.

   1 Which of the activities on the left do you think he probably enjoys?

   2 🔘 1 Listen. Tick the ones he mentions.

2 Listen again. What else does he say about ...?

   • why he enjoys these things   • how often he does them

   Compare in pairs. Then check with the Tapescript on *p.106*.

3 Which of Magnus's leisure activities do you think would be difficult for a blind person? Why? What sort of person do you think he is?

Vocabulary

Having fun

1 Tick the things in the circle you enjoy regularly.

2 Tick the sentences you agree with.

SAYING HOW YOU **FEEL**

THINGS I LIKE		THINGS I DO		THINGS I DON'T DO	
1 I really enjoy dancing.	☐	**6 I occasionally like to** go to a classical concert.	☐	**9 I don't really like** the Beatles.	☐
2 I love jumping off the diving board in the swimming pool.	☐	**7** I go to the pub **whenever I get a chance**.	☐	**10 I'm not very keen on** sport.	☐
3 Science museums these days **are great**.	☐	**8** I like to go camping **whenever I get the time**.	☐	**11 I'd quite / really like to** go up in a hot-air balloon.	☐
4 Golf **is a great way** to relax.	☐				
5 The Beatles **are** still **one of my favourite** groups.	☐				

3 Use the phrases in **bold**. In pairs, how many interests do you share?
I really enjoy playing the guitar.

4 What do you think of these six suggestions? In pairs, take turns to read out the suggestions. Reply from the **Yes / No** box below.

What about going to the pub?

1 — There's a dry-ski slope near here. **Why don't we** go skiing?

2 — **Let's** go into London for the day.

3 — **I think we should** hire a car and go into the country.

4 — **We could always** go away somewhere for the weekend.

5 — **What about** just going out for a meal together?

6 — **How about** cooking something ourselves, together?

YES	NO
That's a nice idea.	It's a nice idea, but ... (I can't drive).
That's a great idea.	Oh, it's too ... (far / complicated / expensive).
Yeah. Let's do that.	Mmm, I don't really like ... (skiing).
	I don't really feel like it.

5 What can you do where you are now? Agree on what to do together.

Infinitive and gerund

1 What are infinitives and gerunds? Match the items.

A	B	C
1 I can	a to drive.	i = gerund
2 I really enjoy	b drive.	ii = infinitive with *to*
3 I'd like	c driving.	iii = infinitive without *to*

2 Translate sentences 1, 2, and 3. Do you use all three forms in your language?

> **Infinitives and gerunds are ways of using verbs.**
>
> We usually use a verb to describe that an activity or event happens:
>
> **I live** in Barcelona.
> **We play** tennis every weekend.
> **Pieter drives** to work.
>
> But sometimes we want to make a <u>comment</u> about the activity / event so we use the infinitive or gerund.
>
> <u>I don't like</u> **living** in Barcelona.
> <u>I'd like</u> **to play** tennis more often.
> <u>I can't</u> **drive**.

3 Complete these phrases.

A
1 go (ski)   *skiing*
2 go (shop)   _____
3 go (fly)   _____
4 go (camp)   _____

B
5 You might even (find) _____ something valuable.
6 Many companies can (take) _____ you up in a two-seater plane.
7 Your local tourist office will (give) _____ you details.
8 I think we should (hire) _____ a car.

C
9 I really enjoy (dance) _____ .
10 I love (jump) _____ off the diving board.

D
11 I occasionally like (go) _____ to a classical concert.
12 I like (go) _____ camping whenever I get the time.

E
13 I'd quite like (go) _____ up in a hot-air balloon.
14 I'd really hate (go) _____ rock climbing.

F
15 Why don't we (go) _____ skiing?
16 Let's (go) _____ into London for the day.

G
17 What about (go) _____ out for a meal together?
18 I'm not keen on (cook) _____ for other people.

4 Look again at groups **A** to **G**. Match them to the descriptions below.

A go ...	
☐ prepositions (*about* / *on* ...) ☐ some verbs of feeling (*like / love / enjoy / hate* ...)	+ gerund
☐ *like / love / hate* when you mean 'I sometimes do it'. (*I often like to have a swim.*) ☐ would + *like / love / hate* ...	+ *to* + infinitive
☐ *Let's ... / Why don't we ...? / Why not ...?* ☐ modal verbs: *can / could / will / would / may / might,* etc.	~~*to*~~ + infinitive

🕐 ## Against the clock!

5 Set a time limit
Finish the sentences with a verb in the infinitive or gerund.

1 I'm not interested in ...
2 I wouldn't like ...
3 I don't want to go ...
4 I hate ...
5 I occasionally like ...
6 I'm not really very keen on ...
7 I shouldn't ...
8 Let's ...
9 This evening, why don't we ...
10 This weekend, I think I'll ...

6 Now relax. Compare with a partner.

> **Learn grammar through vocabulary**
>
> When you are trying to learn grammar rules, collect and learn phrases which contain the grammar.
>
> • Make a note of phrases which say things you want to say.
> • Write them in groups according to their grammar. If you can remember which group they are in, you will remember the grammar rule.

English in use
Getting information

1 Gilly is phoning the tourist office in Boston. Look at her notes. Make questions.

What's the weather like in late August?

2 🔊2 Listen to her conversation.

  1 What four things does she ask about?

  2 Listen again. What information does the clerk give her?

  3 What would you do in Boston?

3 🔊3 Listen to Gilly again.

  1 Complete these phrases.

    1 I'm thinking of coming over to …

    2 I was wondering if you could give me some general information about …

    3 I was wondering if you could tell me …

    4 with regard to swimming, do you …

    5 Regarding hotels, should I …

  2 Listen again and repeat. Copy the intonation.

  3 Test each other in pairs. Give your partner the first word. If they can't remember the whole phrase, give them the second word and so on.

  4 In pairs, practise with your own endings.

  I'm thinking of coming over to Tours next …

4 Look at Tapescript 🔊2 (*p.106*).

  1 Complete the list of expressions in the **Active listening** box.

  2 What words and phrases (and noises!) do you use in your language?

5 Roleplay conversations between a tourist and a clerk.

  CLERK Decide where you want to give information about, e.g. your own city / area, or somewhere you have been.

  TOURIST Decide what questions you are going to ask. Make notes like Gilly's.

Active listening

Gilly and the clerk use expressions like *OK / Oh, fine,* etc. These phrases help conversations go well. They mean 'I'm listening / I understand'.

1	OK	5	_____
2	Oh, fine	6	_____
3	_____	7	_____
4	_____	8	_____

Remember
- Use the vocabulary for leisure activities you've practised.
- Remember to use infinitive and gerund forms correctly.
- Try to use expressions for getting information.
- Practise including phrases to say *I'm listening* and *I understand*.

Speak out
Travel agents

1 In groups, choose a holiday destination. Plan a holiday. Use these ideas.

evening activities   **location**   likely weather

type of customer (age/s, families, etc.)

accommodation   places to visit   **cost**

special events (e.g. barbecues)

sports activities   other …?

2 Find a partner from another group.

  1 Tell your partner the location of your holiday.

  2 Find out as much as you can about your partner's holiday. Would you like to go there?

05
A QUESTION OF LIFESTYLE

In this Unit

- Learn how to give indirect answers to questions.
- Practise using comparatives of adjectives and adverbs.
- Look at vocabulary for describing daily routines, lifestyle, and health.

Speaking
Lifestyle

1 In one minute, tick things from the circle that are important in your life.

2 What's missing? Add one or two words that describe your lifestyle.

3 In pairs, ask questions about your partner's choices.
What do you mean by 'fun'?
Why is 'work' important to you?

Reading
The biological clock

1 When do you do the things on this 'time line'? Write the times. Compare in groups.

sleep	8 hours' work / school	free time
go to bed	get up	finish work / school	go to bed

2 True (✓) or false (✗)? Complete the 'You' column.

Opinions	You	The article
Young children like getting up early.	☐	☐
Teenagers have trouble getting up in the morning.	☐	☐
Teenagers are lazy.	☐	☐
Teenagers don't function well if they get up early.	☐	☐
School should start later for teenagers.	☐	☐

3 Read the article.
1 What opinions does it give? Complete the chart in ex.2 above for 'The article'.
2 What reason do the researchers give for their ideas?
3 Underline five new words or phrases in the article to remember. Then cover the article. Use the words and phrases to explain your own opinion.

Are teenagers lazy?

Teenagers who don't get up in the morning are brighter and more successful.

A study of students' sleep by researchers in the USA found that teenagers who get up early are often tired and can't concentrate in class.

'Young children love to get up early but teenagers have a different biological clock,' says Dr Mary Karskaden of Brown University, Rhode Island. Her research showed that teenagers naturally go to sleep and wake up later than normal – for good biological reasons.

Now many American schools have changed the start of their morning classes from 7.30 to 8.30 or even 9.00.

One teacher said, 'When school began at 7.25, half of the students were almost asleep for the first hour. Since we changed to 8.30, the kids are more active and they are learning more.'

Daily Mail

Listening
Vox pop*

* A lot of ordinary people's comments recorded in a list.

1 What advice have you heard about these things?

   1 What time should people go to bed?

   2 What's the best amount of sleep to have?

   3 What causes insomnia?

   4 What should you do if you can't sleep?

2 Listen to people answering the four questions.

   1 How many answers can you hear?

   2 In pairs, how many answers can you remember? Listen again and check.

3 Listen again and complete.

   1 _An early night is_ better for you.

   2 It's better to sleep …

   3 Just sleep when …

   4 I would like to have about …

   5 … would be nice.

   6 They say, for old people, it's about …

   7 The best amount of sleep to have is …

   8 I think you function better on … rather than …

   9 The more you sleep, the more …

   10 I can't go to sleep if I'm …

   11 I get up and …

4 Complete the phrases with your own opinions. Do you all agree?

Vocabulary
Routines and health

1 **Against the clock!** In groups, make a list like this of everyday activities. The first group to reach 20 shouts 'Stop!'. Read out the list.

Morning	Afternoon	Evening / night
wake up have a cup of tea / coffee		

2 Group the phrases from the box in a spidergram like this.

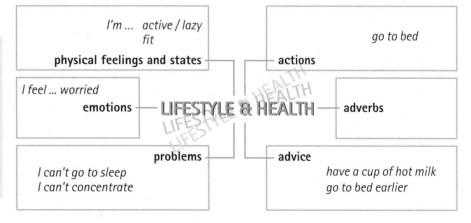

3 Close your book. How many phrases can you remember?

4 Do a Health Questionnaire. In pairs, turn to _p.99_.

Vocabulary tip

Make spidergrams.

• Use phrases so that you remember the word AND how to use it.

• Put words together with similar or opposite meanings. If they have an order, put them in order.

• When you've made a spidergram, put it away and try to write it again from memory.

I'm <u>always</u> <u>tired</u>
I can't re<u>lax</u>
a<u>void</u> <u>co</u>ffee and tea
have a health check
I can't wake up
un<u>healthy</u>
do more <u>exercise</u>
go to sleep
<u>early</u>
a<u>sleep</u>

<u>guilty</u>
a<u>wake</u>
stressed
un<u>fit</u>
<u>healthy</u>
<u>cheerful</u>
wake up
late
get up

Comparatives of adjectives and adverbs

1 In pairs, compare yourselves.

  1 Which of you is ...?

    taller / shorter   older / younger
    fitter / less fit   darker / fairer

  2 And which of you is ... ?

    more / less ... | active   careful about food
                  | serious   interested in health

  3 What is the difference between the adjectives in **1** and the adjectives in **2** above?

2 Think of some more differences between you.

  1 Put the adjectives in the correct column below.

Comparative adjectives	
...-er	**more ...**
tall short fit old	active careful
young dark fair	serious interested

  2 Tell another partner about the differences you have discussed.
    Juan is taller than me.

3 Compare the lives of people today / 150 years ago.

  1 Tick the sentences that you think are true.

	T / F	Adj / Adv
a Life is harder these days.	☐	
b People work harder these days.	☐	
c Most people lived longer then than they do now.	☐	
d Most people are healthier than they were then.	☐	
e Most people had better food then, but less of it.	☐	
f These days, everyone tries to do better all the time.	☐	

  2 Change the false sentences to make them true.

  3 Which sentences have adjectives and which have adverbs? Write *Adj* or *Adv*.

Comparative adverbs		

Many comparatives can be used with verbs or with nouns, i.e. the adjective and adverb form is the same.

  + verb   I can **work better** in the evenings.
  + noun   My **concentration** is **better** in the evenings.

The most common are:

good **better**	hard **harder**	late **later**
soon **sooner**	bad **worse**	fast **faster**
long **longer**	a lot / much **more**	far **further**
slow **slower**	early **earlier**	little **less**

Other adverbs take *more* or *less*:

  more / less ... | easily   carefully   cheerfully
                   | efficiently   strongly

I can **work more easily** in the evenings.
BUT My **work** is **easier** this term.

⏱ Against the clock!

4 **Set a time limit** ▭
Complete these sentences.

  1 Everything is (fast) *faster* and (efficient) _____ these days.

  2 We do everything (fast) _____ and (efficient) _____ these days.

  3 People were (happy) _____ then because they accepted things (easy) _____ .

  4 People enjoyed life (a lot) _____ in those days.

  5 People had (bad) _____ housing, (bad) _____ medicine, and (little) _____ fun a hundred years ago.

  6 Things are getting (good) _____ all the time, but people think they're getting (bad) _____ !

  7 In the past, people started work (early) _____ and finished (late) _____ than we do.

  8 These days, we can travel (far) _____ and (quick) _____ .

5 Now relax. Think of three more differences. Use a comparative in each one.

6 Who do you think live longer – tall people or short people?

  1 In pairs, **A** turn to *p.100*, **B** to *p.103*. Read your article. Remember what it says. Don't make notes!

  2 Compare what you have read. What is the truth, do you think?

  3 What changes can we make to our lifestyles to live longer? List your suggestions. Then compare your ideas with the class.

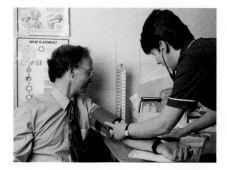

English in use
Being indirect

1 Add three more things in each column. Compare in pairs.

Things I should do more	Things I should do less / I shouldn't do
exercise eat fruit and vegetables read	eat chocolate smoke watch TV / videos

 2 Listen to Will having a health check. Complete the chart.

	How much?	OK / not OK?	Do you believe him?
smoking			
drinking			

3 Complete these extracts from the conversation.

Nurse Are you a smoker?

Will   ¹*Not really* , no, um, I, I do occasionally smoke a cigar and it ² _____ comes to ³ _____ one a month.

Nurse Are you tempted to smoke more, sometimes ?

Will   Um, ⁴ _____ , ⁵ _____ .

Nurse Do you drink any alcohol on a regular basis?

Will   ⁶ _____ an awful lot. Um. At the moment I'm probably having a drink every day.

Nurse Just one?

Will   ⁷ _____ glasses of wine.

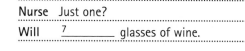

about
a couple of
I suppose
it varies
~~not really~~
occasionally
probably

 4 Listen again and check. Translate phrases 1 to 7.

5 Listen and repeat the phrases. Copy the intonation.

6 Practise being indirect.

  1 Make questions. Complete the answers so they are true for you.

    1 … ? Not really.

    2 … ? It probably comes to about …

    3 … ? Occasionally, I suppose.

    4 … ? It varies a lot.

    5 … ? I'm probably having …

    6 … ? A couple of …

  2 In pairs, ask about alcohol, smoking, and diet. Answer with indirect expressions.

Being indirect

Very often, we want to say that something is only **partly** true, or **not exactly** true, or **possibly** true, or **approximate**. We use:

* a few useful phrases
  not really / not exactly / sort of

* intonation and noises
  um / er / well, etc.

Speak out
Make a vox pop

1 In groups, make a vox pop on one of these topics.

  1 Choose a topic. Think of three questions to ask about it, e.g.

    • What do you do to … (stay healthy / get on with people)?

    • What's the best way to … (have fun / relax)?

    • What advice would you give about … (being healthy / having fun)?

  2 Interview three or four people each. Note their answers. Collect similar answers together.

2 Perform your vox pop. Read out the answers your group collected.

Remember

* Use some of the vocabulary you've looked at for talking about lifestyle and health.

* Try to use comparative forms correctly.

* Practise giving indirect answers.

06
CHANGE OF STATE

In this Unit

- Practise vague expressions of time and quantity.
- Talk about things you used to do.
- Learn vocabulary for talking about similarities and differences.

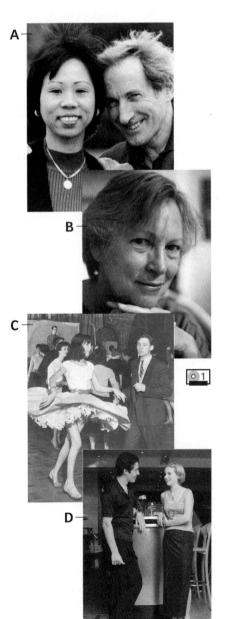

A

B

C

D

○ 1

Speaking
Someone similar

Who, in your family, is most similar to you and who is most different from you? Tell your partner. Think about the kind of ...

things you enjoy doing   people you like   clothes you wear
things you talk about   music you like   things you find funny

Vocabulary
Similarities and differences

1 Complete the sentences to describe people in photos A to D.

– (no word)	as	between	from	in	that	to	too	very

1 He's completely different _from_ her.
2 They're quite similar _____ each other in age.
3 I think she's _____ young for him. She'll get bored with him.
4 They've got a lot _____ common.
5 I think they're quite a good couple: they look _____ similar.
6 The single woman looks quite like _____ the older man – except _____ she's a woman of course!
7 There are so many differences _____ them: they'll split up before long!
8 She looks about the same height _____ him.

2 Write these words under the correct sound. Listen and check.

~~bored~~	young	quite
<u>couple</u>	be<u>tween</u>	com<u>ple</u>tely
height	like	each
be<u>fore</u>	<u>other</u>	<u>shor</u>ter

/iː/	/aɪ/	/ɔː/	/ʌ/
see	why	door	up
		bored	

3 Look at the /ə/ sound (schwa) in these words.

similar = /sɪmɪlə/	common = /kɒmən/	different = /dɪfrənt/

1 Is /ə/ stressed or unstressed?
2 ○2 Which words from ex.2 have a schwa? Listen and check.

4 Compare the couples in the photos.
1 Which couple is most similar and which is most different? In what ways?
2 Is it better for couples to be similar or different?

Reading
Marrying and living abroad

1 Match the phrases.

1	They're an elderly	e	a	-in-law.
2	I like my mother-	☐	b	marriage: she's French, he's Indian.
3	Shshsh! Don't disturb	☐	c	ever go out.
4	We hardly	☐	d	country.
5	We live in an apartment	☐	e	couple.
6	They have a mixed	☐	f	block.
7	Visit a foreign	☐	g	the neighbours!

2 Which event is the most difficult? Why?

- if you retire
- if you move to a foreign country
- if new neighbours move in next door
- if you marry someone of a different nationality

3 ⏱ **Against the clock!** In pairs, read the beginning of this article and decide in five minutes ...

1 Which photos on *p.24* look like Eunice and Ann?
2 What have they got in common?
3 How many differences can you find between them?
4 What do you think the rest of the article will be about?

4 Read more about Eunice and Ann. In pairs, **A** turn to *p.100*, **B** to *p.103*.

5 Compare the two women.

1 What other similarities and differences do they have?
2 How would you feel in their positions?
3 How would you feel about marrying someone from a different culture?

Marrying someone from a foreign country is seldom easy. **Annie Youngman** reports

A world apart, together

'It's difficult here. I find I am living in the 1940s, not '90s. It's too quiet, not like Singapore.'

Eunice Jackson, 37, moved from Singapore to England 18 months ago with her husband, John. They have been married for four years.

'If the family came to stay, it was absolutely not allowed to ask when they were leaving.'

Ann Phiri, 57, moved to Lusaka with her Zambian husband, David. They were together for 24 years but have recently split up.

The Guardian

Talking about 'usually' in the past

1 Which sentences describe **a** one event, **b** more than one event, **c** a period, **?** not clear?

1 I met my husband in Singapore. — a
2 We lived there for two years. — ☐
3 We moved to England 18 months ago. — ☐
4 When my sister was here, I told her to keep quiet! — ☐
5 When I was in England, we went shopping in London. — ☐
6 We went shopping in London on Saturdays. — ☐
7 We rarely went out. — ☐
8 I loved chocolate as a child. — ☐

2 Read the **Past simple** box. Check your answers.

Past simple

The past simple can describe:

1	a single event	I **met** my husband in Singapore.
2	more than one event	We rarely **went** out.
3	a period	We **lived** there for two years.

It is usually obvious which you mean, but sometimes you need to use an expression of frequency:

What did you do in England?
We went shopping in London.
What, once?'
No, we went **every Saturday morning**.

---

3 Think of a long holiday you've had.

1 Remember some things that you did ...

- once
- every day
- three times or more
- often

2 In pairs, ask questions about your holidays.

4 Read Gemma's memories of when she was a child.

'I'd get up first and wake up Sam, my brother. We'd have to keep quiet because our Dad would be asleep at that time and we were frightened of him. We'd get dressed and go outside and play, and then when it was time, we'd walk to school.

Dad worked nights, so the evenings were wonderful. Mum and Sam and I would have dinner in front of the fire and then we'd play and talk until bedtime. Mum would tell us stories and she'd stay with us until we fell asleep.'

1 What word is *'d*? Write the full form.
2 Describe the beginning and end of your day when you were a child.

---

would

We use *would* to describe frequent routines and actions in a previous period of life / times gone by. It is usually used with actions: *get up, wake up, get dressed*, etc.

  I'd get up first and wake Sam.

It can be used with states (*be asleep, be tired, know, understand*) IF they are part of a routine.

  Dad **would be asleep** at that time.

---

5 Look at these statements.
  1 Which are true for you?
   As a child ... **1** I used to be shyer than I am now.
          2 I didn't use to eat much.
          3 I used to have much longer hair.
          4 I used to hate going to bed.
          5 I didn't use to like school very much.

  2 [○3] Listen and repeat.
  3 Make five questions to ask your partner.
   Did you use to be shyer than you are now?

---

used to

We use *used to* to say that something was normal in a previous period of life / times gone by.

  • actions   I **didn't use to** eat much.
  • states   I **used to** have longer hair.
  • situations We **used to** live in a flat (but now we live in a house).

In questions and negatives it is pronounced the same, but spelt *use*:

  I **didn't use to** eat much.   **Did** you **use to** be shyer?

Remember, the *to* is pronounced with a schwa /ˈjuːstə/.

---

6 Think of an example of any of these things that you particularly remember. Add any that are missing. Tell a partner about them.

games you used to play	food
Saturday or Sunday mornings	going to school
things you'd do with friends	grandparents
things you were afraid of	
things that adults used to say	

Listening
Friday nights 1950 to 1990

1 Look at the photos of going out on Friday night. What differences are there between the 90s and the 50s? Think about ...
  • the kind of people   • clothes   • music
  • what people did / do   • the atmosphere

2 Tick things which are true for young people in your country.
  ☐ Most people go to clubs to listen to the music.
  ☐ A lot of young people go to the cinema.
  ☐ People go out to be with friends and talk.
  ☐ The big attraction is the opposite sex. Boys go to pick up girls and girls pick up boys.
  ☐ People spend most of the time on the dance floor just dancing.
  ☐ The point is to enjoy a lot of different experiences; not to go just to one club, but a couple.
  ☐ People go for the atmosphere on the streets: the music, the colours ...
  ☐ Clothes are very important. People's outfits are like a kind of uniform.

3 Listen to a radio programme about Friday nights in Birmingham.

1 Which bits are about the '90s and which bits are about the '50s? Tell your partner each time it changes.

2 Listen again. Which topic **don't** they talk about?
- music
- clothes
- the Friday night routine
- food
- the atmosphere
- picking up a partner

3 Check with the Tapescript (*p.107*). Find one thing they say about each topic.

4 Which would you prefer, Friday nights in the 1950s or the 1990s?

English in use
Vague expressions of time and quantity

Vague expressions

time

about	eight nine o'clock
round about	by	-ish

quantity

| lots of | a few | a couple |

frequency

| normally | most of the time |
| mainly | usually |

1 5 Listen and complete these phrases from 4.

1 You'd go out *about* five o'clock.

2 ... and then _____ five-thirty six _____ , the road would fill up with people.

3 You'd _____ get home _____ midnight.

4 The evening starts about _____ o'clock.

5 We _____ just spend _____ on the dance floor.

6 The whole point of going out ... is to enjoy _____ different experiences.

7 You go to _____ of clubs, and maybe _____ different bars.

8 I used to _____ wear circular skirts.

2 6 Listen and repeat. Copy the intonation.

3 What about you? Ask in pairs. How different are you?

1 **About** what time do you **usually** go out on a Friday or Saturday night?

2 What do you **normally** do **round about eight-thirty nine-ish** on a weekday?

3 When you go out for the evening, what do you spend **most of the time** doing?

4 Do you **normally** get home **by** midnight?

5 What sort of clothes do you **mainly** wear when you go out?

6 When you go out, how many places do you **normally** go to?

4 Which topic gives you the strongest emotional memories?
- differences: between couples / foreigners / countries
- childhood experiences
- a night out in the city

1 List all the new words or phrases from this Unit about that topic.

2 Put them in the order you would use to describe your experience.

3 Describe the experience vividly to your partner.

Vocabulary tip

Your memory is biological and more emotional than logical. Use it to help you remember experiences.

- Collect words and phrases which describe a powerful atmosphere or an experience that was important to you.

- Put them into an order which means something to you.

Speak out
Making a radio programme

How have you changed as you've grown up?

How have people's lifestyles changed in home life / work / leisure?

What's the best change that has ever happened to you?

In groups, plan a radio programme about differences between the past and now.

1 Choose <u>one</u> question to ask everyone in the class.

2 Ask your question round in the class. Note the answers.

3 Return to your group. Put the answers into a logical order.

4 Prepare an introduction and a conclusion. Perform your programme.

Remember

- Use vocabulary for talking about similarities and differences.

- Use *would* and *used to* to describe past experiences.

- Include at least four vague expressions for time and quantity.

07
TAKING CHANCES

In this Unit

- Practise expressions for agreeing with someone.
- Focus on linking ideas to explain 'why'.
- Extend your vocabulary for describing activities and feelings.

Speaking
Dangerous activities

1 Which of these activities have you done / would you like to do?

driving	motor-racing	playing rugby	smoking
fishing	mountain climbing	scuba-diving	
hang-gliding	parachuting	skiing /ˈskiːɪŋ/	

2 What is your current number one favourite activity? Why?

Reading
Finding information

1 Look at these words. Find ...
  1 four health issues
  2 two things in the home
  3 one sport

injuries	badminton	cancer
toothpaste	curtains	
heart disease	car accident	

2 ☀ **Against the clock!** Write as many activities as you can in each group in one minute. Which of the groups do you think is riskiest?

ADVENTURE SPORTS	ORDINARY SPORTS	EVERYDAY ACTIVITIES

3 Read the article. What do you find most surprising?

What are the riskiest sports you can do? Well, if you thought of 'dangerous sports' like hang-gliding, parachuting, or scuba-diving, you'd be wrong, because they're not, in fact, that dangerous.

According to recent statistics, the sport that causes most injuries is rugby, and football is a close second. Despite the popularity of these games, and although we teach school children to play them, they injure more people per 1,000 than motor-racing, skiing, or scuba-diving.

Of course, people do get hurt in 'adventure sports' and the most dangerous is climbing, which kills eight people a year. But it is not always obvious which activities are dangerous. For instance, two people die every year in hang-gliding accidents, but the same number are killed by badminton, whereas six people a year die in fishing accidents! So 'exciting' isn't always the same as 'dangerous'.

This is even more true when you consider the activities of everyday life. Many more people die due to accidents in the home than from sports of any kind. Did you know that 160 people per year are killed by toothpaste and 3,600 are killed by curtains (although how this happens is a mystery)! And if you really want to live dangerously, then have a cigarette, or get in a car, because the three biggest killers in the UK are heart disease, cancer, and car accidents, in that order. So to live longer, stop smoking, sell the car, and start jumping out of aeroplanes! ■

4 According to the article, which is the most dangerous in each group?

A	**B**	**C**
football	badminton	cancer
motor-racing	climbing	car accidents
rugby	fishing	curtains
scuba-diving	hang-gliding	heart disease
skiing		toothpaste

EXCITEMENT

RISK

0   5   10

5 Ask a partner about their activities. Mark their lifestyle on a diagram like this. How would they like to change it?

Linking

because / although / despite, etc.

1 Make eight correct sentences.

1 Adventure sports are popular …
   - because   **a** the excitement they offer.
   - because of   **b** they're exciting.

2 A lot of people smoke …
   - although   **a** they know it's bad for them.
   - despite   **b** knowing the risks.

3 Some people get injured …
   - due to   **a** they haven't been trained.
   - because   **b** inadequate training.

4 Some people get injured …
   - in spite of   **a** they are very experienced.
   - even though   **b** being experienced.

2 Put these expressions into two groups.

~~despite~~	although	because	in spite of
even though	because of	due to	

+ clause	
+ noun or *-ing*	*despite*

Using linking expressions

because / although / even though are followed by a clause.

   I love climbing **because it's exciting** / **although it's dangerous**.

because of / due to / despite / in spite of are followed by a noun or *-ing* form.

   I love climbing **because of the excitement** / **in spite of knowing** the risks.

Notice that the clause / phrase with the linking expression can come first.

   Although it's dangerous, I love climbing.
   In spite of knowing the risks, a lot of people smoke.

3 Complete with seven different linking expressions.

1 *Because* hang-gliding is dangerous, you need to learn how to do it properly.

2 Rugby is still a popular game _____ it's dangerous, and _____ a lot of people get injured.

3 _____ needing lots of expensive equipment, and _____ the many accidents, more and more people are going climbing.

4 People do dangerous sports _____ the excitement: the enjoyment is _____ the risks involved.

 Against the clock!

4 Set a time limit
In pairs, make true sentences. Use as many linking expressions as you can.

1 I enjoy / I don't enjoy team games …
2 I think / I don't think adventure sports are good …
3 I drive / I don't drive fast …
4 I've had / I've never had an accident …
5 I smoke / I don't smoke …
6 I have / I don't have an active lifestyle …

A

B

C

Listening
Listening for opinions and feelings

1 Look at the photos. What are they doing?

2 🔲1 Listen to three conversations.
  1 Match them with the pictures.
  2 Which person is describing …?
    ☐ a school trip
    ☐ an adventure holiday
    ☐ a trip with a company called *Real Dreams*

3 Listen again. Who felt like this? When?

embarrassed	excited	exhausted	nervous
involved	miserable	relaxed	terrified

4 Tick the sentences you agree with. Who are you most similar to?
☐ Life is too safe these days.
☐ Facing physical danger increases your confidence.
☐ Everyone should experience danger at some time.
☐ Adventure activities are pointless and stupid.

English in use
Finding agreement

1 Do you usually try to agree with … ?

a man	a woman
your guest / host	someone much older or younger than you
someone you are attracted to	a 'superior', e.g. your president / boss

2 🔲2 Listen to extracts from the conversations again.
  1 How do they agree each time? Choose the correct phrase.

1 We're so safe these days and life is so easy	Yeah, that's true	No, that's true
2 And I don't think it's good for us	Yes, so do I	No, nor do I
3 We need the chance to develop confidence	Yeah, I agree	No, I agree
4 You just can't get that experience in everyday life	Yes, that's right	No, that's right
5 I think everyone needs to have that experience	Yes, so do I	No, nor do I
6 I don't much like walking really	Yes, so do I	No, nor do I
7 I hate it	Yeah, me too	No, me too

  2 🔲3 Listen and agree.

3 Practise agreeing with these comments.

  1 Lovely weather we're having.
    Yes, lovely, just like last year.
  2 I don't like this music.
  3 I think we're out of petrol.
  4 That was great. I really enjoyed it.
  5 I don't think much of the bus service.
  6 Look out! That idiot! I hate drivers like that!
  7 Look! Oh, I'd love to do something like that.

Agreeing

We use a variety of ways to agree with other people's statements.

- **Agreeing with a positive statement**
  Yes / yeah / So do I
- **Agreeing with a negative statement**
  No / Nor do I
- **Agreeing with positive or negative statements**
  that's true / me too
  that's right / I agree

We also use strategies for agreeing with someone.

- **Repeating what someone says**
  'Life's so easy.'
  'Yeah, that's true, it is easy …'
- **Supporting what someone says with another example**
  'I don't like walking.'
  'No, nor do I, especially up mountains.'

  'I think everyone needs to have that experience.'
  'Yes, so do I. I get the same sort of thing from skiing.'

Vocabulary
Describing emotional reactions

-ed and -ing endings

Most -ed and -ing adjectives are derived from verbs:
excite – exciting / excited

- -ed adjectives describe your feelings.
  I'm excited about going to Thailand.

- -ing adjectives describe experiences.
  It was exciting being in Thailand.

Be careful: many verbs do not form adjectives in this way, so you have to find a different way to say what you mean (e.g. NOT I was very **concentrated**. BUT I was very **involved** OR I **concentrated** very hard.)

1 Complete the gaps with -ed or -ing adjectives.

1 embarrass-   Everyone feels _embarrassed_ about something.
               English people find wages very _____ to talk about.

2 excit-   It's the most _____ thing I've ever done.
               I felt so _____ .

3 exhaust-   I've never been so _____ .
               It looks really _____ .

4 frighten-   It's the most _____ film I've ever seen.
               There was a time when I was really _____ .

5 relax-   I've never been so _____ .
               It's the most _____ thing I do.

6 involv-   It's the most _____ activity I can think of.
               You get totally _____ in it.

2 Why are these wrong? What should you say?

1 I was very boring.
2 I was so embarrassing.
3 Are you exciting?
4 You look totally exhausting.
5 I feel frightening.

3 Talk about how you feel.

1 Put these adjectives into groups in the chart. Mark the stress.

confused	excited	surprised	embarrassed
exhausted	frightened	involved	miserable
relaxed	interested	happy	bored
emotional	violent	confident	attracted (to someone)

	Good feelings	Bad feelings	Neither good nor bad
I often feel			
I don't often feel			

2 Find out when your partner has those feelings and why.

Vocabulary tip

Make a note of new words by writing them in groups:

- water sports / air sports / team sports / hunting
- things I like / things I don't like
- ordinary activities / unusual activities / in-between activities

Speak out
The dream experience

1 Write on a piece of paper an experience which you think everyone should have in their life. Change papers with another group.

2 Imagine you own the company 'Real Dreams'. Choose one or two experiences. Plan trips to give people those experiences. Make notes under these headings.

| DESTINATION | DURATION | THE EXPERIENCE | FEELINGS | BENEFITS |

3 Describe your trips to other groups. Which trip sounds the best?

Remember

- Try to use linking expressions as you describe your trips.
- Include a wide variety of vocabulary to talk about activities and feelings.
- As you listen to other people, practise using agreeing expressions.

08
GETTING THROUGH?

In this Unit

* Practise using 'telephone English'.
* Make future arrangements with *will*, *going to*, present continuous.
* Talk about the effects of the phone on our lives.

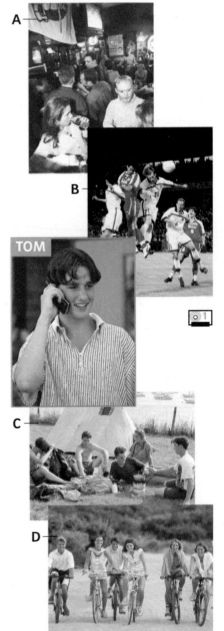

A

B

TOM

C

D

Speaking
Making contact

1 How do you most like 😊 / least like 😞 to contact people?

1 Tick the chart.

	a stranger	a friend	your parents	someone special
send an e-mail				
send a post card				
write a letter				
phone				
meet face to face				

2 Compare in groups. Explain your choices.

2 ⏱ **Against the clock!** In pairs, **A** turn to *p.100*, **B** to *p.103*. Explain your phrases. Which pair can finish first?

Listening
A busy social life

1 In pairs, what do photos **A** to **D** tell you about Tom's social life?

2 Tom calls two friends, Gareth and Nick. Listen.
  1 Which two pictures go with Call 1? ☐ and ☐
  2 Which two pictures go with Call 2? ☐ and ☐

3 Listen again. Complete Tom's notes about the two calls.

> Gareth – football
> Gareth → pub with _____
> Will call me back around _____ .

> Nick – camping
> Meet in the _____ at
> _____ p.m.
> Bring _____ .

4 What do they say about these? Check with the Tapescript on *p.108*.
  * Mike
  * Laura
  * cycling

5 List five things that you've done with friends. Talk about your lists.
  When did you last go (*camping*)?
  * Where did you go?
  * Who with?
  * What happened?
  * What was it like?

Future arrangements

1 Look at these sentences from Tom's phone calls. Match them with their uses (**a** to **d**) from the **Making arrangements** box below.

1 **Are you watching** the game tonight? ☐ a

2 **Are you going to watch** the football tonight? ☐

3 (Mike) **is finishing** work at five and then **he's going to give** me a call. ☐

4 **I'll call** you back later, **shall I?** ☐

5 **I'm just about to** go home now. ☐

6 Well, **I'll give you a call** there then. ☐

Making arrangements
We use several different tenses to talk about the future.

a	arrangements you already have	= present continuous / going to
b	suggestions	= will and shall I ...?
c	guarantees	= will
d	the very next thing you're going to do	= (be) about to

2 Look at this sentence.

D'you   you're gonna
~~Do you~~ know where ~~you are going to~~ go?

1 [○ 2] Listen and repeat three sentences.

2 Contract these sentences in the same way.

1 Are you going to go out this evening?
2 What are you going to do?
3 I will meet you there, shall I?
4 Do you know where you are meeting them?
5 I am just about to have dinner.

3 [○ 3] Listen, check, and repeat.

Against the clock!

3 **Set a time limit**
In pairs, imagine and complete this conversation.

A _____ this evening?

B Well, yes, in fact. _____ . Would you like to come?

A Oh, yes, that would be great. Where _____ ?

B Well, _____

A Uh huh. And what sort of time _____ ?

B

A Right. So, I'll _____ ?

B

A

4 Now relax. Change partners. Have a similar conversation. Make an arrangement for this evening.

5 Practise making arrangements.

1 Make a diary like this. Write down three things you're doing over the next seven days.

8 Monday	Thursday 11
9 Tuesday	Friday 12
10 Wednesday	Saturday 13
	Sunday 14

2 Think of four or five other things you would like to do with people in the class.

3 Now make arrangements with as many people as you can. Fill your diary.

Vocabulary
Telephone phrases

1 Match these phrases.

1	make / have	b	a	on	
2	call / phone / ring	☐	b	an arrangement	
3	speak	☐	c	to someone	
4	hold	☐	d	someone	
5	answer / get	☐	e	calling?	
6	Give me	☐	f	call	
7	make a phone	☐	g	phone	
8	she's on the	☐	h	a ring / a call.	
9	Who's	☐	i	the phone	

Vocabulary tip
There are thousands of word combinations to learn in English.

- Collect word combinations as you meet them. Write 'matching' tests.
- Test yourself, or work with a friend and test each other.

2 Cover each side. Say the whole phrase. Test a partner.

3 Look at these phrases.

1 Which ones are said ...   **a** by a person   **b** by a machine?

   a If you know the **extension number** you require, please **dial it** now.

   b If you need assistance from **the operator, please hold.**

   c For credit card bookings, **please press one.**

   d **Can you hold,** please?

   e I'm **putting you through** now.

   f Hello, **you're through to** Credit Card Bookings, **can I help you?**

2 Translate the phrases in **bold**.

English in use
Guiding a phone call

<table>
<tr><td colspan="2">

We use standard expressions and responses to guide the stages of an informal phone call.

1 Answer the phone

| Gareth | **Hello.** |

Say hello

Tom	Hi, Gareth. It's Tom.
Gareth	Hello Tom.
Tom	How are you doing?

2 Discuss arrangements

Tom	Are you watching the game tonight?
Gareth	**Sorry?**
Tom	Are you going to watch the football tonight?

Finish arrangements

| Gareth | **All right then.** |
| Tom | Fine. |

3 General chat (about Laura)

4 End the phone call

| Gareth | **Anyway,** I'll give you a call later, yeah? |
| Tom | Excellent. |

Say goodbye

Gareth	All right then, **see you later.**
Tom	See you. Bye.
Gareth	Bye.
</td>
<td>

1 🔆 **Against the clock!** In groups, what phrases do people use on the phone? Which group can write the most phrases in five minutes?

2 In pairs, look at the **Expressions and responses** box.

1 What do the phrases in **bold** mean? Write them in the **Expressions** column.

		Expressions	Responses
a	Who's that?	= *Hello.*	*Hi. It's ...*
b	What did you say?	=	
c	Let's finish talking about that.	=	
d	I'm ready to end the phone call.	=	
e	Say goodbye.	=	

2 Now write the response which comes after each expression.

3 Complete the gaps in Tom's next call. Then check with the Tapescript on *p.108*.

Answer the phone

Nick's mother	Double five three six four oh
Tom	Hi, *can I speak to* _____ Nick, please?
Nick's mother	Yes, _____ ?
Tom	_____ Tom.
Nick's mother	Oh, _____ Tom. How _____

Getting Nick

| Nick's mother | I'll _____ . Hold _____ . |
| Tom | Thank you very much. |

End the call

| Tom | OK. See you later. |

Say goodbye

Nick	See _____ .
Tom	Bye.
Nick	_____ .

4 🔲 Listen and repeat. Copy the intonation.
</td></tr>
</table>

Yes and no

Notice several different ways of saying 'Yes' and 'No'. Note that it can sound rude to say just 'no' to a suggestion.

OK, Right, Fine, Excellent, Great

I don't know, I'm not sure

---

5 Look at the postcard from Adrien.

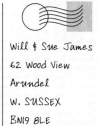

We are coming down to Bognor on the evening of Saturday 23rd, staying until the Tuesday or Wednesday – any chance of getting together? We'd love to see you all again.

Lots of love
Adrien

Will & Sue James
62 Wood View
Arundel
W. SUSSEX
BN19 8LE

1 You'd like to see them but can't make the 23rd. Think of a suitable reply suggesting a meeting.

2 In pairs, sit back to back. Roleplay the phone call.

PHONE POWER

When I asked my daughter (16) which item she would keep: the phone, the car, the cooker, the computer, the TV, or her boyfriend, she said 'the phone'. Personally, I could do without the phone entirely. Which makes me unusual. Because the telephone is changing our lives more than any other piece of technology.

Point 1 The telephone creates the need to communicate, in the same way that more roads create more traffic. My daughter comes home from school at 4.00 pm and then spends an hour on the phone talking to the very people she has been at school with all day. If the phone did not exist, would she have anything to talk about?

Point 2 The mobile phone means that we are never alone. 'The mobile saved my life,' says Crystal Johnstone. She had an accident in her Volvo on the A45 between Otley and Skipton. Trapped inside, she managed to make the call that brought the ambulance to her rescue.

Point 3 The mobile removes our privacy. It allows Marketing Manager of Haba Deutsch, Carl Nicolaisen, to ring his sales staff all round the world at any time of day to ask where they are, where they are going, and how their last meeting went.

Point 4 The telephone separates us. Antonella Bramante in Rome says, 'We worked in separate offices but I could see him through the window. It was easy to get his number. It was a very passionate seduction – but we didn't meet for the first two weeks!'

Point 5 The telephone allows us to reach out beyond our own lives. Today we can talk to several complete strangers simultaneously on chat lines (at least my daughter does. I wouldn't know what to talk about). We can talk across the world. We can even talk to astronauts (if you know any) while they're space-walking. And, with the phone line hooked up to the computer, we can access the Internet, the biggest library on Earth.

Reading
Never alone with the phone

1 How many ways can you use the phone system?
local calls, the Internet ...

2 Read 'Phone Power'. Find examples from the article of how the phone, **a** improves our life, and **b** makes it worse.

3 How does the phone affect your life?

Speak out
Making phone calls

1 In groups, look at the mobile phone pictures.

1 Who could be speaking to whom? What are they talking about?

2 Suggest five or six phrases or sentences they might be saying.

2 In pairs, make up a phone conversation.

1 Choose two of the photos.

2 Make up the conversation between them and practise it.

3 Perform it or record it for the class.

Remember

- Include some of the language you've practised to talk about social activities.
- Use the correct tenses for making future arrangements.
- Try to include as many telephone phrases and responses as you can.

09
INCIDENTS AND ACCIDENTS

In this Unit

- Practise expressions for responding to good / bad news.
- Look at present continuous, *going to*, *will*, and present simple for planning the future.
- Learn vocabulary for special occasions.

SEASON'S GREETINGS?   ...No thanks!

Oh no! Christmas again. More than birthday parties, more even than wedding receptions, Christmas is, above all, the occasion I hate the most. And why? It's hard to say which is worse: sending cards to people you never see; visiting relatives you can't stand; eating and drinking more than you want; presents for children who would be nicer people if they had less; obliged to spend money you don't have; and the weather is always dreadful. The list of complaints against Christmas is endless – so why do we do it?

Speaking
Celebrations

1 What occasions have you celebrated in the last two years?

2 In groups, read the article.
   1 What doesn't he like about Christmas?
   2 Do you agree with him?

3 Are there any occasions you particularly like or hate? Explain why.

Vocabulary
Special occasions

1 What types of occasion are Groups **A** and **B**?
   1 How many can you add to Group **A**? Say what they celebrate.
   2 In Group **B**, order the occasions. Explain your order.

Group A
Christmas
Divali (Hindu Festival of Lights)
Hsien Nien (the Chinese New Year)
I Shawwal (the end of Ramadan)
Kodomonohai (the Japanese festival, Children's Day)

Group B
a birthday
a wedding
a bereavement
the birth of a child
an engagement

2 On which occasions do you do these things? Add to the lists.

have	invite	
a <u>fun</u>eral	<u>rel</u>atives	go to church
a <u>par</u>ty	a few close friends	send cards
a pro<u>ces</u>sion	all your friends	give <u>pres</u>ents
a reception	<u>neigh</u>bours ·	let off <u>fire</u>works
a <u>nam</u>ing ceremony	<u>colleagues</u>	

3 Make phrases.

1	enter / win / lose	b	a	an arm / leg
2	take / pass / fail		b	a compe<u>ti</u>tion / race
3	break		c	an <u>acc</u>ident / a <u>job</u> interview
4	get		d	job
5	get a		e	an e<u>x</u>am
6	have		f	engaged / <u>married</u> / di<u>vorced</u>

1 Which ones have you done? How did you mark the occasion?
2 Which ones do you think you will do?

4 Choose up to ten words / phrases to learn from this section. List them in alphabetical order. In pairs, try and say them all.

Vocabulary tip

We often remember what sound a word begins with.

- Try listing new words and phrases in alphabetical order.
- Put the list on the wall next to your bed, in the bathroom ...
- Read the list every time you pass it.

Listening
Incidents and accidents

1 How do these people feel?

I've passed.   I've won.   I've failed.

I've lost.   I've got an interview.   I've had an accident.

2 When these happen to a friend, what do you say in your language?

3 Listen to six conversations.

1 What is the occasion each time? Number 1 to 6.

job interview ☐   wedding ☐   accident ☐
exam ☐   birthday ☐   thank you ☐

2 Listen again. Say what's happening / has happened.

3 In pairs, what details can you remember? Check with the Tapescript on *p.108*.

4 Choose a similar occasion that has happened to you. Say what happened, what you did, and how you felt.

English in use
Phrases for special occasions

1 Match situations 1 to 8 with 'Occasion expressions' **a** to **h**.

1 It's Christmas!   [*f*]   5 I didn't get the job. ☐
2 I'm going to my brother's birthday party. ☐   6 I've passed my exam! ☐
3 It's been lovely having you to stay. ☐   7 I've broken my arm. ☐
4 I'm going for a job interview tomorrow. ☐   8 I've just got engaged. ☐

2 Listen and check. Then repeat. Copy the intonation.

3 When can you answer with these expressions? Practise in pairs.

And a Happy New Year!	Have a good time.	What a shame!
I really enjoyed it.	That's great!	Bad luck.
I hope it goes well.	Brilliant!	How awful!

4 **Against the clock!** In pairs, cover all the expressions. Remember what to say in each situation. Say and respond as many times as you can in two minutes.

5 Practise exchanging news.

1 Complete the sentences. Imagine one of them has happened to you.

It's my _____ today.

I've just heard my _____ 's sick.

I've got an exam _____ .

I've just been offered a _____ .

I've _____ all my exams.

I'm getting married _____ .

2 Walk around. Say hello to everyone, and pass on your news. When someone gives you their news, respond, then ask one or two questions about it.

Occasion expressions

a Congratulations!

b Well done!

c Oh dear! How did it happen?

d Oh, I am sorry.

e Well, thank you very much indeed for having me.

f Merry Christmas!

g Enjoy yourself!

h Really? Well, good luck!

Notice, that for really tragic news, for example a bereavement, we say *I'm really sorry* or *I'm terribly sorry*, but we have nothing else special to say. What you say depends entirely on your relationship.

Planning the future

YOU ARE INVITED TO A BALL AT
THE CHALFONT HOTEL
TO CELEBRATE THE 21ST BIRTHDAY OF
SARAH DIXON

~ four course dinner ~ live jazz band & dancing

7.30 PM – 2.00 AM

DRESS FORMAL   RSVP

1 Look at the invitation.

   1 What's the party going to be like? Make four predictions.

   2 Would you like to go to a party like this?

2 Are these people going? Say 'Yes', 'No', or 'Maybe'.

Matt Not really my style, is it? I mean, it's going to be very posh: look at the invite.

Sarah I'm going with Rajit. He's going to get two days off work for it.

Helen Why not stay at my place? I'll pick you up at the station.

Mike Really? Well I'll come then. Thanks Helen.

Robin I don't think I'll be able to. I think I'll be in the States, at a conference. I hope not, but I'll just have to see.

Finn Oh, we won't miss it. Maria and I will be there, no question!

Maria I'm in Thailand the day before, but I'm going to get there all right – believe me, I'll be there!

Present continuous, *going to, will*

Names	Types of future	present continuous	going to	will/won't
1 *Sarah*	it's already arranged	✓	✓	
2	I know from present evidence		✓	
3	I intend to do this		✓	✓
4				
5	promises / guarantees / offers / requests			✓
6	sudden decisions			✓
7	uncertainty: hopes / fears / possibilities with *think* / *probably*			✓

This chart shows how to express different types of future.

3 Look at the people's comments in ex.2 again. Write their names in the chart.

Present simple

We use the present simple to express the future if it's part of a written / formal plan or timetable.

   My plane **leaves** at 6.00 a.m.

4 Which person comments using the present simple for future? Why?

5 [○3] Listen and repeat the comments. Copy the intonation.

Note

We write *I am going to* … but we say *I'm gonna* … /ɡənə/

Against the clock!

6 Set a time limit

In pairs, complete the conversations. Compare your answers with another pair. Correct any mistakes.

1 **A** What (you / do) <u>are you doing</u> this evening?

   B (I / go) _____ out. Would you like to come?

   A Where (you / go) _____?

   B Don't know – I'd like to go to the theatre – but (I / probably / end up) _____ in the pub!

2 **A** What (you / do) _____ for Christmas?

   B Don't know.

   A (you / stay) _____ here?

   B Yes, I'm afraid so. It's too far to go home.

   A Well, why don't you come and stay with us?

   B What? For Christmas?

   A Yes. (There / only / be) _____ me, my sister, and my Dad. (you / be) _____ welcome.

   B All right. Then (I / come) _____. Thank you very much.

3 **A** Oh no! Look at all this traffic. (We / be) _____ late.

   B Why don't we go round the other way?

   A I don't think (it / help) _____.

   B Well, (I / ring) _____ them – I've got my mobile here.

   A Oh, good idea.

7 Now relax. Listen to your teacher and check.

8 Find out about your partner's future. Choose from 1 to 4.

A What are you doing / What are you going to do for Christmas?

B I'm going to stay with my family / I'm staying with my family.

I don't know, but I think I'll stay with my family.

1 Ask about plans this year.

this weekend
for your next birthday
for Christmas
for your next holiday

2 Ask about ambitions and intentions in life.

travel
live abroad
try and get rich
get married
have kids
retire

3 Ask for predictions about what's going to happen.

to you
to your English
in your country
in the world

4 Make plans to meet up in the future.

A Invite your partner to a celebration or festival next year.

B Think of problems: nowhere to stay, travel, cost, wife / husband / girlfriend / boyfriend

A Offer to help with the problems.

B Decide to go.

Speak out
A class reunion

1 Imagine that it is one year from now. You are attending a class reunion. By yourself …

1 Think of two or three things that have happened to you over the past year.
2 Think of one or two special occasions you have been to.
3 Think of a reason why you have to leave the reunion early.
4 Also imagine that one of these things has happened to you.

Remember
- Try to use a variety of tenses correctly for talking about the future.
- Respond to good and bad news with appropriate expressions.
- Include vocabulary for special occasions.

You are getting married (or re-married!). You are thinking of moving.

You've had a baby (or another one). You are thinking about what kind of future it will have.

You've broken your leg. You'll be able to run again in about five weeks.

You've won £10m. You are thinking about what to do now.

The company you work for has closed and everyone has lost their jobs, including you. You are not sure what's going to happen.

It's your birthday today and you still haven't decided how to celebrate it!

Your company wants you to change jobs and move to Siberia, for more money. You've got three weeks to decide. If you don't go, it'll be bad for your career.

You've won a trip to a space station. If you don't want to go, you can choose someone else to go instead.

You have failed an important exam. You don't know what to do now.

2 Now get up and join the party. Say hello to everyone, and find out what's happening in their lives. Try to talk to everyone.

10 OTHER HOUSES, OTHER RULES

In this Unit

- Use sentence patterns with *because / otherwise / so / when,* etc.
- Practise expressions for obligation and permission (*must / have to,* etc).
- Learn vocabulary for rules and arguments.

Speaking

Rules

1 Answer this questionnaire by yourself.

A QUESTION OF ATTITUDE	Are your attitudes the same as your country's? Write **T** (True), **F** (False), or **?** (maybe).
MY COUNTRY	**ME**
Rules aren't important – nobody follows them anyway.	
Rules are necessary, even if they're sometimes inconvenient.	
Many of our national heroes are rebels.	
It's important to follow the rules because it shows respect.	
It's often exciting to break the rules.	
We only have rules because some people love having authority.	
People like rules – that's why we have them.	

2 In groups, compare your answers. If you disagree, find out why.

Vocabulary

Time for an argument

1 Think of situations in your life when there are a lot of arguments.

2 ⏱ **Against the clock!**

   1 In pairs, define these words. **A** turn to *p.100* and help **B**, **B** turn to *p.104* and help **A**. Which pair can finish first?

A puddings	mealtimes
the main course	the washing-up
dinnertime	unfair

B annoying	interrupted
on time	arguments
got upset	banned

   2 Finish each sentence with one word / phrase.

     1 In my family, nobody liked *mealtimes*.
     2 The whole family met at ...
     3 I didn't often like ...
     4 but I always loved Mum's ...
     5 Nobody helped Mum with ...
     6 which I think was very ...
     7 Nobody got to the table ...
     8 And everyone always ...
     9 which caused terrible ...
     10 and someone always ...
     11 Mum said we were very ...
     12 So talking at dinner is now ...

3 Complete the sentences with these phrases.

argue	to argue
us argue	us arguing
arguing	

   1 We mustn't ...
   2 They don't let ...
   3 We're never allowed ...
   4 They spend all their time ...
   5 They always stop ...

4 Use the expressions to talk about your family / work / school, etc.
My boss lets me / doesn't let me ...

Vocabulary tip

The card method is an effective way of learning a lot of vocabulary quickly.

- Make a pack of 20 word cards. Put one word or phrase on the front of each card. On the back, put a sentence with the word missing.
- Look at each sentence. If you can say the missing word, put the card at the bottom of the pack. If not, look at it and put it in just a few cards later, then try again.
- Then look at the words and try to remember the sentences.

Listening
Home rules

1 Alice and Colin have six children aged two to 16. What sort of rules do you expect them to have? Think of four or five examples.

2 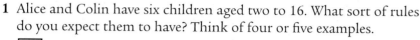 Listen to the family talking about the rules in their house.

  1 Number the topics in Column A in the order they talk about them.

A	B
☐ helping with the washing-up	a If you're not here when we're ready to start, then you don't get pudding
☐1 arriving on time for meals	b You mustn't interrupt when somebody's talking – you've got to wait till they've finished
☐ rules in friends' houses	c After dinner, we've got to help with the washing-up, 'cause with eight of us, there's a lot to do
☐ talking at mealtimes	d Television is banned in the week and they're only allowed to watch it at weekends
☐ watching the news on TV	e You don't let us watch the news, even at weekends
☐ when they can watch television	f The trouble is, they're reaching an age where nobody else ever has to do the washing-up ...

  2 Match Column **A** with Column **B**. Listen again and check.

  3 Remember anything else they said. Check with the Tapescript on *p.108*.

3 In groups, how similar are your answers?

  1 What was it / is it like in your house?

  2 If you had six children, would you have the same rules?

English in use
Sentence patterns with *because / otherwise*

1 Read the 'Rules for behaviour', and 'Reasons'. One reason is generally positive and one is generally negative. Write + or – each time.

Rules for behaviour	Reasons	+/–
1 Everyone has to work	because everyone needs money.	☐
	otherwise you don't have any money.	☐
2 You've got to have some fun	because that's what life's all about.	☐
	otherwise life's miserable.	☐
3 You mustn't steal	because it's dishonest.	☐
	otherwise you might get caught.	☐
4 Don't spend more than you earn	because that's basic good sense!	☐
	otherwise you'll get into debt.	☐

2 Which word do we use for, **a** negative, **b** positive reasons?

Note

You can also put *otherwise* at the end of a sentence.

*Don't spend more than you earn because you'll get into debt **otherwise**.*

We often use sentences in patterns.

1 **the occasion** After dinner,

2 **the rule** we've got to help with the washing-up,

3 **the reason** because with eight of us, there's a lot to do,

4 **comment** but it's a bit annoying if you've got things to do.

Other common words introducing patterns are *when / if / so / and.*

When you're studying for an exam / you should go to bed early / **so** you feel fresh the next morning / **and** you'll be able to concentrate better.

| *If* you're going to travel by tube, you have to buy a ticket before you get on a train _____ you can be arrested and fined. _____ you need a ticket to get through the gates anyway _____ it's quite hard to forget!

3 Think of positive and negative reasons for these rules.

1 You have to do exercise sometimes …

2 You should wash regularly …

3 You've got to make friends …

4 Number the phrases in order using the sentence pattern in the box.

1
- [ ] otherwise it causes arguments
- [ ] and it's quite annoying when someone keeps interrupting you
- [ ] the rules at the table are that
- [ ] you mustn't interrupt when somebody's talking

2
- [ ] they're only allowed to watch TV at weekends
- [ ] our biggest arguments are about television
- [ ] because they're lucky to live in the countryside
- [ ] and if you send them outside, they quickly find something to do

5 Read the 'Rules for travelling on the tube'.

1 Complete the text with the following words.

| and | because | but | if | otherwise | so | when |

2 **○2** Listen and check your answers. Is Rule 3 an official rule?

3 **○3** Listen and repeat. Copy the intonation.

2 _____ you first go into a tube station, _____ you need to ask for directions, then you have to go to the ticket office. _____ , buy your tickets from the machines, _____ it's much quicker.

3 _____ you're on the train, you mustn't look at anyone else, _____ you certainly mustn't talk to anyone, _____ everyone is very suspicious of everyone else. _____ you can read _____ look at the adverts and maps!

6 Think of the rules for two situations in your life. Tell a partner.

At what age can I …?

5 You have to go to school!
You have to pay to go on trains, buses, etc.
You can drink alcohol in private – for example at home.

10 You can be convicted of a criminal offence.

12 You can buy a pet.

13 You can get a part-time job, but you can't work for more than two hours on a school day or on a Sunday.

14 You can go into a pub but you can't buy or drink alcohol there.

Reading
Finding specific information

1 How old do you have to be to do these things in your country?
- [ ] go to school
- [ ] drink alcohol
- [ ] leave school
- [ ] marry
- [ ] drive
- [ ] vote
- [ ] pay on public transport
- [ ] buy cigarettes
- [ ] work for money

2 ☀ **Against the clock!** In pairs, read the text in five minutes. Find out when you can do the things in ex.1 in England and Wales.

3 Which age restrictions are unfair? Why? Compare in pairs.

16 You can leave school.
You can marry but you must have your parents' consent.
A boy can join the armed forces with his parents' consent.
You can buy cigarettes and tobacco.
You can have beer, cider, or wine with a meal in a restaurant.

17 You can have a licence to drive most vehicles.
You can go to prison.

18 You reach the 'age of majority' – you are an adult in the eyes of the law.
You can vote in elections.
You can open a bank account.
You can buy alcohol in a pub.

21 You can become a Member of Parliament.

The Guardian / Children's Legal Centre

Obligation and permission

1 Complete from 'At what age can I ...?'

1 You **can** have a driving licence when you are __17__ .

2 You **can** go to prison when you are ____ .

3 You **can't** vote until you are ____ .

4 You **have to** go to school between the ages of ____ and ____ .

5 You**'re allowed** to leave school when you are ____ .

6 You **can** get married at ____ but your parents must ____ .

7 Children **mustn't** go into pubs under the age of ____ .

2 Translate the words in **bold**. Are they the same in your language?

3 Look at these expressions.

I can ...	a I must ...
I can't ...	b I'm allowed to ...
I have to ...	c I mustn't ...

1 Match the similar meanings.

2 Use the six expressions to describe your life at the moment. Tell a partner.

---

can, have to, must, be allowed to, should, need to

~~to~~ + verb	to + verb
You **can** drive	You**'re allowed to** smoke
You **must** have a licence	You **have to** follow the rules
You **should** go to bed early	You **need to** sleep

Notice:

I **don't have to** work. = it's not necessary
You **mustn't** drive over 70. = it's important NOT to

---

4 Read the text.

Of all the ages you can be, I like mine the best.

And why?

Firstly, because **I don't have to work**. I don't even **have to get up** in the morning if I don't want to.

And secondly, nobody asks me stupid questions like 'How are you getting on with Margery?' or 'How's the job?'. Nobody ever listens to the answers anyway – they only ask because **they think they should**.

And yes, I do have a job – I am a writer. A night writer. I write from 10.00 pm until 4.00 am, every night. **You don't need much sleep** at my age but people don't like it: they seem to think that **people of my age shouldn't stay up** after eleven o'clock!

What do I write about? Why, the silly social rules that **people have to follow** between 10 and 65. **I shouldn't laugh**. But it does makes excellent material for books.

1 Complete these sentences.

1 He likes being retired because he doesn't have to ...

2 People only ask about your partner because ...

3 He can stay up till 4.00 because old people ...

4 People seem to think that old people ...

5 People between 10 and 65 have to ...

6 But people under 10 and over 65 ...

2 Cover the text. Say the sentences from memory.

5 Describe some of the advantages of being your age. Use all the verbs in the **Language** box on the left.

Speak out
Write the rules

Remember

* Include some vocabulary for rules and restrictions.

* Use sentence patterns to describe a rule, what it's for, and what you think of it.

* Try to use *can*, *have to*, *must*, *should*, etc. correctly.

1 In groups, read the article. Why do people join clubs?

2 Choose a club. Write the Club Code.

1 Explain briefly who the club is for and what it does.

2 Write up to seven rules for the members.

3 Explain your Club Code to the class.

CLUBS – WHY?

Martin Frankl wonders about clubs and societies

Why do people join clubs? Is it the sense of belonging that it gives? Do the clubs organize competitions and conferences? Can they even provide a career in your hobby? Does membership offer reduced prices for equipment and activities? Is organization necessary to get people to change the world? Or is it just because people love rules? Because, where there is a club or society, there is a Rule Book.

Apathy Society (The)	Fine Wines and Foods	New World Group (The)
Computer Games Workshop	Fun Club (The)	Philosophy Circle
Conversation Club (The)	Gardening Association (The)	Shoppers' Society (The)
Cosmetics Club (The)	Guns & Firearms Club (The)	Star Trek International
Credit Card Group (The)		Teenage Action on Rights
Dangerous Sports International	Islamic Society (The)	Under 30's Club (The)
	Letter Writers' Circle (The)	Vegetarian Society (The)
	Mongolian Society (The)	Volleyball Society (The)
		Women's Group (The)

Speaking
Feelings

1 In groups, how many emotions can you think of? Write a list of feelings and how they affect you.

anger   *you shout and scream, you shake, you go red, ...*
fear   *you ...*

2 Talk about when you felt one of the emotions. What happened?

English in use
Complaining

1 Where are these problems likely to happen?

a bar/pub/café	a hotel	a restaurant	a shop	a station

Problems	
the wrong change *in a shop/bar, etc.*	a dirty cup/spoon
the wrong size dress/shirt	a cracked glass/plate
the wrong ticket	a damaged CD/cassette/book
a dirty room/a noisy night	horrible coffee/beer/food
a delayed journey	a faulty cassette recorder/camera

2 What do you do if you have a problem like this? Tick the chart.

What do you do?		How do you do it?	
complain to the staff	☐	get upset and look unhappy	☐
ask the staff to put it right	☐	get angry	☐
ask to see the manager	☐	be friendly and cheerful	☐
do nothing – forget it	☐	be polite but serious	☐

3 Which of these solutions would you accept for the problems above?
the wrong change = *an apology*

an apology	a refund	change it

 4 Listen to two conversations. Complete the chart.

	where	the problem	the solution	helpful staff?	calm customer?
1	*a café*				
2					

Simple complaints

When staff are helpful, problems can be solved immediately. Simple complaints usually have three parts.

1 Attract attention
Excuse me

2 Explain the problem
I'm afraid (this camera is faulty).

3 Say what you want
I'd like (a refund), **please**.
Can I have (another one), **please?**
Could you (change it), **please?**

Difficult complaints

When someone is unhelpful, you have to insist. Follow the stages for simple complaints, and then ...

1 Sympathize
I understand / I realize / I appreciate (that)

2 Repeat your request
but / however ... I want (to change it)

3 Acknowledge the problem
... even though (I haven't got the receipt)

It's important to keep calm, and not get angry!

ANGER

JACQUI BRADLEY, 27, IS A TEACHER.

I don't lose my temper very often but when I do, I really explode ...

People say it's good to get your anger out, but my problem is that I don't get angry enough. If I said something immediately, I could stay calm. Instead, I wait, getting more and more irritated until I lose control. *Woman's Realm*

---

5 Read **Simple complaints**.

1 Find the three parts in Conversation 1.

A Um, excuse me.

B Yes?

A I'm afraid this coffee's cold.

B Oh, I'm sorry.

A I'd like another one, please.

B Yes, of course.

A Thank you.

2 How else could you say *I'd like another one*? Use the phrases in the box.

3 🔲2 Listen and repeat. Copy the intonation.

6 Read **Difficult complaints**. Complete these two conversations.

1 A Excuse me, I bought this yesterday, and _____ it's too big. _____ to change it, please.

B Have you got your receipt?

A _____ not, no, but I've got the bag and everything.

B I'm sorry but we don't change things without a receipt.

A Well, I _____ that, _____ I want to change it, _____ I haven't got the receipt.

2 C I'd like a refund, please.

D I'm sorry, it's not our policy to give a refund.

C I _____ that, _____ I want a refund, _____ it's not your policy.

D I'm sorry, I can't do that. We're not allowed to.

C Well, _____ speak to the manager, please.

7 Practise the conversations from memory with a partner.

Listening
Losing your temper

1 Look at the article about Jacqui.

1 What's happening in the cartoons?

2 What do you think Jacqui would do in these situations?

2 🔲3 Listen to Jacqui talking about 'one of those days'.

1 Explain how these things come into her story.

- a puddle of water
- six o'clock
- the pavement
- a borrowed dress
- door keys
- a drain

2 Did Jacqui go to the party in the end?

3 Read about something else that happened to Jacqui.

1 In pairs, **A** turn to *p.100*, **B** to *p.104*. Work out what happened.

2 🔲4 Listen and check. Were you right? What do you think of Jacqui's behaviour?

4 Describe something similar that has happened to you or to someone you know. Use some of these words and phrases.

lose my temper	explode	irritate me	get fed up	have a tantrum
lose control	go mad	get irritated	stay calm	be angry

Narrative tenses

1 Look again at extracts from Jacqui's stories.

> 1 — I **woke up** to find a huge puddle of water on the floor. So I **cleared it up** and **was late** for work.

> 2 — The friend I **was meeting** irritated me because **she'd forgotten** to bring back a dress **she'd borrowed**, which **I'd planned** to wear to a party that night.

> 3 — I **was** in a queue and the assistant **was going through** some papers and **ignoring** us. A pregnant woman **was** obviously **having difficulty** standing for so long.

1 Look at the phrases in **bold**. Write the extract numbers by each tense, **a** to **c**.

  a the past simple ☐

  b the past continuous ☐

  c the past perfect ☐

2 Match the tenses **a**, **b**, **c**, with their uses **i**, **ii**, and **iii**.

  i being in the middle of an action

  ii things that happened earlier

  iii the main events of the story

Compare three past tenses for stages in a narrative.

Past simple

One event after another
He **drove** up to the house and **jumped** out.
Activities together
We **had** breakfast and **talked** about it.

Past continuous

One activity 'containing' a shorter one
I **was working** in Berlin when we met.
A 'long' activity leading up to an event
It **was raining**. A car slowed down and stopped.

Past perfect

Earlier events
I **hadn't seen** him for years but I recognized him immediately.
When I got to the door, I realized I**'d forgotten** my keys.

---

2 In pairs, match each sentence with **a** or **b**.

  1 It was a cloudy morning. ☐

  2 It was a beautiful day. ☐

    a The sun was shining through the window.

    b Then the sun shone through the window.

  3 James had breakfast. ☐

  4 James had had breakfast. ☐

    a His dirty dishes were still on the table.

    b Then he cleared the table.

  5 I knew he was leaving ☐

  6 I knew he had left ☐

    a because the house was silent.

    b because I could hear the door opening.

---

  7 I got to work late. ☐

  8 When I got to work ☐

    a he'd called, and left a message.

    b Then he called me and explained.

  9 He said he was doing a job for the police ☐

  10 He said he'd done a job for the police ☐

    a a few years before but not any more.

    b and he had to go abroad for a few weeks.

  11 When I got home, the police had called ☐

  12 When I got home, the police called ☐

    a and asked me where he was.

    b and left a note asking me to call them.

  13 That night, James was saying goodbye ☐

  14 That night, James said goodbye ☐

    a and left.

    b when the police arrived and took him away.

3 Decide on a title for the story. Read the sentences again and choose one from each section. Then cover and tell a different partner your story.

⏱ Against the clock!

4 **Set a time limit**

In pairs, read this true story and complete with the past simple, past perfect, and past continuous.

There's an **axeman** in my bedroom!

Sinead woke up. A man (stand) ¹ *was standing* at the end of the bed. She (think) ² _____ that her boyfriend, Richard, (get up) ³ _____ for a drink. But then she (realize) ⁴ _____ that Richard (lie) ⁵ _____ next to her. 'My God', she (scream) ⁶ _____ . Richard (wake) ⁷ _____ up. The man (come) ⁸ _____ closer. He (hold) ⁹ _____ something: an axe. 'He's going to kill us!' Richard shouted and threw himself at the man. Sinead heard the two men hit the floor. Then she (hear) ¹⁰ _____ a scream in the next room: her nine-year-old daughter, Jenna. 'Get her out, Sinead,' Richard shouted. Sinead (shake) ¹¹ _____ with fear. She (move) ¹² _____ to the door, but the axeman (stand) ¹³ _____ in her path. Richard went for the axe and Sinead ran. In Jenna's room, she heard the men crash down the stairs, then silence.

5 Now relax. What happened next? Try to complete the story. Then turn to *p.100*. Find out what happened!

Vocabulary
Occasions and feelings

1 Which have you experienced?
- a funeral
- a religious ceremony
- a riot or revolution
- a festival or celebration
- a wedding

2 These sentences all describe the same colour.

The Ashantis in **Ghana**, in West Africa, use it at funerals. It has a feeling of loss and sadness. It means 'a passing away.'

In **China**, it's the colour of luck and happiness. It's the colour people wear at wedding ceremonies and at celebrations in the New Year.

In **Kathmandu** in Nepal, it's associated with bravery. People also wear it in religious ceremonies.

In **Russia**, in the first years of the Revolution, people wore it proudly for their achievements.

In **Hungary**, traditionally, it was the colour of fire and enthusiasm and of everything that was exciting. But after 1948, after the Communist revolution, it was regarded less favourably because it was the official colour of revolution, which was not very popular.

1 Which colour? What do you associate with that colour?
2 How many words can you find for a events, b feelings?

3 What do you associate with these colours? Think about occasions, feelings, and meanings.
- We use it at …
- It means …
- Traditionally, it …
- It's the colour of …
- It's the colour people wear at …
- It's associated with …

YELLOW	
GREEN	BLACK
WHITE	BLUE

Vocabulary tip

Learn words to describe things which are important to you. Occasions and events are especially good for this as they bring together a lot of ordinary vocabulary which will be useful on many other occasions.
- Look them up and write them down together.
- Group them under headings / in a diagram, e.g. people, places, etc.

---

4 Make a spidergram about an event which was important to you. Write words / phrases which you associate with it. Include:

people
places
activities
objects
feelings

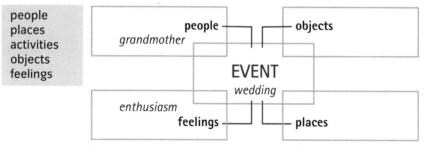

people — objects
grandmother
EVENT
wedding
enthusiasm
feelings — places

5 Cover your spidergram. Remember as many words / phrases as you can.

Speak out
Describing memorable events

1 In groups, choose one of the pictures above, or one of these events:

Complaint!	A fantastic night out	The end of the war	Winning a game

1 Imagine you were there. Describe what happened and what it was like.
2 Together, look up and write the words / phrases you need. Include:
- events: things that happened
- places, sights, sounds, and smells
- feelings

2 In pairs, with someone from another group, describe the event.

Remember
- Use vocabulary for describing moods and emotions.
- Use narrative tenses correctly to say what happened.
- Try to make your experience as vivid as possible.

12
SAYING NO

In this Unit
- Practise making invitations and saying 'no' politely.
- Use infinitives to link words and build sentences.
- Expand your verbs, nouns, and adjectives using affixes.

What do **you** do if someone **invites** you somewhere or asks you a favour and you **don't want to**?

Speaking
Saying no

1 In groups, think of a time when ...
   1 someone invited you somewhere.
   2 someone asked you a favour.

2 Did you do any of these?
   ☐ go even though you didn't want to   ☐ just say 'no'
   ☐ say 'yes' and then not go   ☐ make up an excuse not to go
   ☐ say no and explain why honestly

3 Which of these comments do you agree with? Why?

- It depends who you're talking to, I mean, I can't say no to my parents, but I can say no to people who don't know me very well. **Turkey**

- I'd just say no. If they're your friends, then they'll understand. If they're not, then it doesn't matter anyway. **Spain**

- I would say no, if I don't want to go, and I would explain why honestly, because otherwise, it is impolite, I think. **Japan**

- I think it's important to make an excuse, because otherwise it's too direct. It's impolite just to say, 'No, I won't come.' **Switzerland**

4 There are different social 'rules' in different countries for refusing invitations and requests. What can happen if you get it 'wrong'?

Reading
Reading for the main points

1 In pairs, read the beginning of a magazine article.
   1 How do the British feel about saying 'no'?
   2 What kind of 'tips' do you think the article might suggest?

2 In pairs, read the rest of the article.
   1 **A** turn to *p.101*, **B** to *p.104*. Count the tips. Underline the main words in each.
   2 Tell your partner what tips you can remember.

3 Explain these words from the article.

effective	explanations	body language	'broken record'
firmly	made-up	straighten	calmly
sweetener		reasonable	

4 What tips would you give to people visiting your country?

Vocabulary
Double your vocabulary

1 Split these words into two parts – the base word and the affix.

shortest *short/est*	asking	guilty	reasonable
effective	hardest	kindness	straighten
firmly	impossible	kinder	sweetener

2 Now split these, but add letters to make the complete base word.

refusal *refuse + al*	easier	happily	refusing
psychologist	explanation	politest	

3 ☼ **Against the clock!** In groups, make more words using these affixes in five minutes. Which group can make the most?

-ful	-ity	-ly	-nce	-ness	-tion	im-	in-	un-

friend	happy	important	invite	possible	sensitive	use
friendly						

4 Change the words on the left to complete the sentences.

1 It's very rude to change an *arrangement* just because a better one comes up.

2 It's rude to say 'no' without giving an _____ .

3 It's not your politeness that matters, it's your _____ .

4 In my country, politeness isn't _____ .

5 One thing everybody likes in other people is _____ .

6 It's OK to refuse an _____ without giving a reason.

7 It's _____ to learn to be polite in English.

8 You have to use the right phrases, otherwise people can think you're very _____ .

9 Learning another language perfectly is completely _____ .

5 Look only at the words. Remember the sentences.

arrange (v.)

explain (v.)

sensitive (adj.)

importance (n.)

kind (adj.)

invite (adj.)

use (n.)

friend (n.)

possible (adj.)

Vocabulary tip

Double your vocabulary! When you look up one word in the dictionary, look for related words. That way, you learn two or three words with little more effort, e.g. when you look up *aggression* (n.), you will also find *aggressive* (adj.), *aggressively* (adv.).

Listening
Invitations

1 Look at six things you could be invited to do. What would you expect in your country?

• Are they invitations to someone's home / to go out …?

• Will it be during the day / in the evening / for a whole day …?

• Will you eat / drink anything?

• Will you have to pay for anything?

• Can you take someone with you?

• Will you take something (food / wine / flowers …) ?

2 Listen to five invitations. Make notes like this.

	1	2	3	4	5
Invitation to ...?					
Reply					

3 Listen again. In pairs, note more details. Check with the Tapescript on *p.109.*

4 What's the situation and the relationship in each conversation?

English in use
Invitations and replies

1 Read the text about different styles of invitations.
  1 Do you think this information is true in your country?
  2 What examples of 'elaborate' invitations do you have in your language?

Simple invitations

A simple invitation is usually one short phrase, e.g. *Do you fancy ...?* (informal), or *Would you like ...?* (informal or formal).

Invitation	Reply
1 Do you fancy ...?	I'd love to but I've got to ...
2 Would you like to ... afterwards?	That would be ...

2 Listen to two extracts from 1 again.
  1 Complete the phrases in the box for simple invitations and replies.
  2 Who do you know that you could say these phrases to?
  3 Listen and repeat. Copy the intonation.

Elaborate invitations

Elaborate invitations can include an introduction, an invitation phrase, e.g. *Would you like ...?*, and often a comment, e.g. a description of the event.

3 **Introduce** Look, I was wondering ...
   Suggest Would you like to ...?
   Show appreciation That's very ...
   Accept I'd ...
   Thank Thank you.

4 **Introduce** Hi, Joanna. Look, ...
   Situation We're going to ...
   Invite Would you like to ...?
   Show appreciation Oh, that's ...
   Refuse I'm afraid I ...
   Reason I've got something ...
   Sweetener Maybe another ...

5 **Introduce** Listen, ...
   Situation We're having a ...
   Invite I was wondering if you'd ...?
   Show appreciation Oh that would be ...
   and accept
   Thank Thank you.

3 Listen to three more extracts from 1 again.
  1 Complete the phrases for more elaborate invitations and replies.
  2 Listen and repeat. Copy the intonation.

4 Make invitations and replies.
  • go for a drink   • go out for a meal   • go on holiday with you
  • go for a coffee   • come for dinner   • come round for a barbecue
  • come and see a film   • go camping for the weekend

Looking at 'social' rules

Grammar rules tell you how to make sentences. Social rules tell you what sentences to make, and with whom. Imagine, for example, you really like someone and you say, 'I wondering, if I go party with friends today evening you would like come?' they might laugh at the grammar, but there's a good chance they'll say 'yes'. But if you say, 'You come to a party with me this evening', they may think you are aggressive and arrogant, and say 'no'.

Invitations tend to be simple ...

• if you are talking to good friends

• if you expect the answer 'yes'; or if it's for something small and simple (e.g. having a cup of coffee)

• if you are equal in age and status, and especially if you are both young

Invitations tend to be more elaborate ...

• if you don't know each other well

• if you expect the answer 'no'; or if it's for something large (e.g. going away on holiday) or unexpected

• if you are being formal because you are unequal in age or status, or because you are at a formal occasion, or if you have a naturally formal style

> **Vocabulary tip**
>
> Remember complicated phrases by counting the words.
>
> • Find the longest phrase in the **Elaborate invitations** box. Count the words. Close your book and remember the phrase.

Infinitives

1 Think of one thing that ...

  1 you think is **hard** to do.

  2 is **important** for everyone to do.

  3 at some time in the past, you made **an excuse** not to do.

  4 you think everyone has **the right** to do, or not to do.

  5 you **have** to do this week.

  6 you **should** do more often.

  7 you **must** do while you're young, before it's too late!

  8 you're **going** to do in the next few days.

  9 **makes** you feel good.

  10 you've **asked** or **told** someone to do in the past.

2 In pairs, look again at sentences 1 to 10.

  1 Compare your answers. How similar are you?

  2 Underline the infinitive. Does it follow an adjective, a noun, an auxiliary verb, or a full verb?

Using infinitives

The infinitive is the simplest form of a verb, e.g. *use, go, remember, come,* etc. We use it to attach a verb to other words. It is often used with the word *to*, e.g. *to use, to go,* etc.

adjective + infinitive	It's important **to use** the right words.
noun + infinitive	I don't have an excuse not **to go**.
auxiliary + infinitive	I should **do exercise** more often.
verb + infinitive	She asked me **to come**.

The infinitive has many uses. Here are three common ones.

1 In phrases beginning with *wh-* words (*where, when, who, what*) and *how*.
I don't know **what to say**.

2 With *too* and (*not*) *enough*.
My pasta's **too hot to eat**. / *My pasta's* **not cool enough to eat**.

3 To say why you do something (infinitive of purpose).
I exercise **to keep fit**.

---

3 Underline examples of each use in these sentences. Are they 1, 2, or 3?

  1 My English is<u>n't good enough to talk</u> to English people.

  2 I know what to say but I don't know how to say it.

  3 She talks too quickly for me to understand.

  4 When I'm reading, I use a dictionary to look up nearly every word.

  5 I don't know how to get more speaking practice.

  6 I listen to tapes to get listening practice, but they're too difficult to understand.

4 Complete the sentences.

  1 They've invited me to dinner but I don't know <u>what time to arrive</u> (time / arrive).

  2 I want to go out and have some fun but I don't know _____ (where / go) or _____ (what / do).

  3 I'm getting fat and I'm just _____ (busy / do) any exercise.

  4 I need to find some _____ (people / practise) my English with.

  5 I'm staying with a host family but I can't use the _____ (kitchen / cook) in.

  6 We haven't been together _____ (long / get married) yet.

 Against the clock!

5 Set a time limit ▭

  1 In pairs, find examples of these from 'How to say no nicely' (*pp.48 / 101 / 104*) and 'Looking at social rules' (*p.50*).

wh- / how + infinitive	main verb + infinitive
infinitive of purpose	adjective + infinitive
noun + infinitive	auxiliary + infinitive

  2 Make true sentences with each of the patterns.

---

how to meet people and make friends
how to make successful invitations and requests
how to say 'no'
how to 'fit in' when you go abroad

Remember

- Use ideas from this Unit in your talk.
- Make sure you use the right word form (noun, verb, adjective, etc.)
- Use infinitives correctly to link the words. Check in your dictionary.

Speak out
Preparing and giving a talk

1 Look at the titles of four 'How to ...' articles. What do you think they will say? Suggest as many ideas for each as you can around the class.

2 In pairs, prepare a talk on one of the topics, either seriously or humorously. Use the plan on the right if you like.

3 Work in different groups. Give your talk.

1 Introduction
Explain the importance of doing it well. Give examples of what can happen if you do it badly.

2 Tips
Think of five to ten useful tips. Think of an example for each one. Explain why each is useful.

3 Conclusion
End with a general point.

13
BRAINPOWER

In this Unit

- Learn some communication repair strategies.
- Look at defining relative clauses for giving more information.
- Practise developing your brainpower.

DID YOU KNOW ...?

* People have an average vocabulary of 30,000 words in their own language.

* 'Intermediate' level learners of a foreign language usually have a vocabulary of around 3–4,000 words.

* Before they start speaking at the age of 10–15 months, children already have a passive vocabulary of at least 200 words.

* Between the ages of 1 and 5, a normal child learns, on average, between 8 and 20 new words a day.

* For learners of a foreign language, learning lists of words can be a powerful technique: in one study, Russian learners successfully learned 108 new English words in one go.

Vocabulary tip

Use word association. When you are learning a new word, find a word in English OR in your own language ...

- which looks or sounds similar
- which is related in meaning or comes from the same topic area

The similarity can be very small; it is often enough if the words begin with the same one or two letters.

Speaking
Test your memory

1 Test how good your memory is. In pairs, **A** turn to *p.101* and give the test. **B** close your book and answer **A**'s questions.

2 In groups, decide ...
   1 What types of question are there in the test? Which were the hardest for you?
   2 Is this kind of test useful?

Vocabulary
Word associations

1 Read the 'Did you know ...?' facts.
   1 Do any of them surprise you?
   2 How many ways of learning new words can you think of in three minutes?

2 Look at how words are related.
   1 What is the relation? Tick the correct columns each time.

	have related meanings	often occur together	sound or look similar	same topic
1 short term		✓		
2 short, medium, long				
3 a major event				
4 disk, file, memory, store, erase				
5 store, restore				
6 older, forget, confused, brain cells				
7 permanent, constant, all the time				
8 communication, connections, interconnections				

   2 Explain the meaning of the words in each group.
   3 Can you add words/phrases to any of the groups
     short term *memory*

3 Learn five new words/phrases from this section using word association. Try to remember them at the end of the lesson.

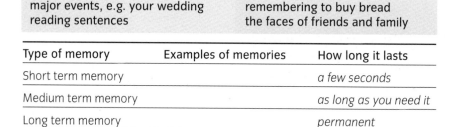

thinking
planning
the intellect

appreciating art
& music
emotions

body clock

balance
movement

Listening
Types of memory

1 What kinds of memory are these? Put them in the chart.

major events, e.g. your wedding reading sentences	remembering to buy bread the faces of friends and family

Type of memory	Examples of memories	How long it lasts
Short term memory		a few seconds
Medium term memory		as long as you need it
Long term memory		permanent

2 [○1] Listen to Lynn and Mick. Check if you were right.

3 [○2] What happens to your memory as you get older? Listen and check what Lynn says about these things.

forget things brain cells dying	learn new things stop communicating	get confused

4 In pairs, describe one short, one medium, and one long term memory.

English in use
Repair strategies

1 [○3] Listen again to Lynn and Mick. What communication problems do they have? Number them 1 to 4.

can't remember the right word(s)	☐
accidentally uses the wrong word	☐
has trouble forming the sentence	☐
doesn't hear / understand	☐

1 **Lynn** So some time later you buy bread, and when you've done it you don't need **to restore, er to store** that memory any longer …

2 **Mick** Are there any …, are …, **are any memories** really permanent?

3 **Lynn** … you start to get confused.
  Mick **Sorry?**
  Lynn You get confused.

4 **Mick** Interconnections?
  Lynn Yeah, **I can't remember the right word, but** that's the problem.

2 When do we use these repair strategies?

1 Say 'Sorry?'
2 Say 'I can't remember / I don't know the right word', then suggest some possible words
3 Say *er/um*, then say the right word
4 Just stop, pause, and start again

3 Describe one of these. Can your partner guess what you are talking about? Use the repair strategies when you have problems.

a job	a machine	a musical instrument	a sport

Reading
Communication problems

1 Look at the quote and the pictures.

  1 What makes a good marriage?

  2 What are the most common problems that husbands and wives have?

2 This is an extract from a novel about a husband and wife.

  1 Explain these phrases to your partner.

my birthday	challenging and triumphant
have an affair	an expression (on your face)

  2 Read the extract. What exactly is the position with Mike, do you think?

"**The secret of a successful marriage?** Concentrate. You gotta concentrate. And remember everything she says."

When Philippa came in, Patrick was looking at the TV. It was a game show.

'Hi. I'm back.'

'Oh. Hi', he said.

'So aren't you going to ask me where I've been?' said Philippa.

'Sorry?'

'I've just been out. Don't you want to know where I've been?'

'Oh, sorry love. Yes, of course. Where have you been?'

'I saw Mike.'

'Mike?'

'You don't remember, do you?'

'Well, I'm sorry.'

'The trouble is,' said Philippa, 'that you're just not interested in anything I do.'

'I am.'

'You've met Mike.'

'Well, I can't be expected to remember all your friends.'

'All my friends! I've been working with Mike for the last year. He's the one I went to Munich with.'

'Oh yes.'

'And the one who remembered my birthday.'

'Oh that. Look, I've said I'm sorry ...'

'In fact, as far as you know, I might be having an affair with him.'

Silence. Then, 'Are you?' he said.

She looked at him in a challenging and triumphant sort of way. He looked at her with a strangely empty expression which very slowly removed all the colour and angles from his face until it looked like an over-boiled potato.

'Well, I think that's the question you have to decide.'

'Sorry?' he said. And turned off the television.

3 What advice would you give to Patrick / to Philippa?

Defining relative clauses

1 Complete these sentences so they are true for you.

  1 When I was younger, I wanted to marry someone who ...

  2 I didn't want to marry anyone who ...

  3 I know a lot of people that ...

  4 I like stories which ...

  5 I don't like films which ...

  6 The best kind of relationship is one that ...

2 Compare in pairs. Underline the relative clauses in your sentences.

3 Complete the rules and examples.

For people, use _____ or _____ .

Isn't that the guy _____ works in the Joyce café?

For things / feelings / events, etc. use _____ or _____ .

Is there anything _____ would make her happy?

I saw something _____ looked like a small elephant.

> ### Recognizing relative clauses
>
> Relative clauses give you information ...
>
> - about **nouns.**   They're major **events that happen in your life.**
>
> - about **pronouns.**   It's **something that I don't want to remember.**
>
> They usually begin with a relative pronoun (*who* / *that* / *which*, etc.).
>
> - *who* is only used for people.
>   *I like people **who** do unusual things.*
>
> - *that* is used for things, events, feelings, animals, and sometimes people.
>   *It's something **that** I don't want to remember.*
>
> - *which* is used for things, events, feelings, animals, etc., but not for people.
>   *It's something **which** I don't want to remember.*

4 Look at how we use relative pronouns.

1 Find the two parts of the sentence. Underline the relative clauses.

1 Long-term memory is like a file / <u>which stores your most important memories</u>.

2 It's a story about a woman who wanted to divorce her husband.

3 There's a road that goes up the hill and behind the wood.

4 The problems that they're having are very common.

5 Can you tell me the three words which I gave you earlier?

6 There's a particular smell I always associate with my grandmother's house.

7 I can remember his voice, but I can't remember anything he's said!

8 I've forgotten a lot about the event, and the things I do remember are all confused.

2 Look at <u>relative clauses</u> 1 to 8 again. Which …?

• have a relative pronoun?
• don't have a relative pronoun?
• need a relative pronoun to make sense?
• don't need a relative pronoun?

Using relative clauses

Relative clauses always follow a main clause. They both need a subject.

Main clause	Relative clause
I remember people	… **who** talk to me.
I remember things	… **which** are important to me.
I remember things	… (which) I enjoy.
I remember people	… (who) I spend time with.

If the relative clause doesn't have its own subject, you must use a relative pronoun.

I remember people … **who** talk to me.
NOT … ~~I remember people talk to me~~.

BUT If the relative clause already has its own subject (pronoun or noun), you don't need to use a relative pronoun.

I remember things **I enjoy.** / **which I enjoy.**

Against the clock!

5 Set a time limit

In pairs, complete with *who*, *that*, or *which*. If the relative pronoun is not necessary, put it in (brackets).

1 Remember everything __*(that)*__ you can about your first class at school as a child: the people, the room, the event.

2 Draw a picture of something small _____ you use regularly, for example, a bank note or a key. How many details can you put on it?

3 Think of a place _____ you constantly go to. Remember five different details about it.

4 Remember the face of someone _____ you've only known for a short time. How many details can you describe (e.g. eyes / hair, etc.)?

5 Think of three problems _____ happen to most married people at some time.

6 Describe something personal _____ is constantly in your memory, such as one of your parents' faces.

7 Name something everyday _____ you can always remember.

8 Remember someone _____ has talked to you today. What do you remember about their voice?

6 Now relax. Write two more tasks. Use a relative clause in each one.

7 Close your books. In new pairs, ask your partner to do as many tasks as you can remember.

8 Remember a scene from early childhood. Think about where it was / when it happened / who was there / what happened / how you felt, and why.

1 Plan your description. Try to use at least five relative clauses.

2 Describe it to your partner.

Speak out
Memory competition

1 Work in fours: **Pair A** and **Pair B**.

Pair A turn to *p.101*. Look at the picture for two minutes.
Pair B turn to *p.104*. Look at the story for two minutes.

2 Exchange information.

Pair A describe the picture to **Pair B** for three minutes. **Pair B** draw the picture.
Pair B tell the story to **Pair A** for three minutes. **Pair A** write the events in order.

3 How many details did you remember? Write the number at the top of your paper. Which team remembered most?

Remember

• As you study the picture / story, think about ways of remembering details for later.

• Use communication repair strategies as you describe and tell.

• Try to use relative clauses accurately.

14
GIVING IMPRESSIONS

In this Unit

- Learn about words for things in general *(thing / stuff / people like that)*.
- Look at *that* clauses for expressing opinions and feelings.
- Practise using words with dependent prepositions.

Speaking
Admirable people

1 Think of someone you admire. Tell your partner why.

2 What kind of people do you most admire? Explain your top three.
- entrepreneurs: people who start out poor and make themselves rich
- people who help other people: e.g. nurses, aid workers, teachers
- great sports people: who push back the limits of what is humanly possible
- people who make a difference: politically, to national success, to world peace
- people who revolutionize science and thought
- rebels who fight against the system (who are often only recognized later)

Listening
Listening for information

1 Put these words into three groups: **School**, **Science**, **People**. Underline the stress.

lazy	(rather) slow	fascinated (by)	the school system
a compass	a patent office	theories	punish
learn by rote	go to lectures	revolutionize	

2 In groups, look at the pictures and text.
  1 What different sides of Albert Einstein's character do they show?
  2 Which group can answer the most questions in three minutes?
     a What is Einstein famous for?
     b Where was Einstein from?
     c What was he like as a child?
     d Where did he study?
     e Was he a successful student?
     f Where did he work?

3 Listen to an extract from a radio programme about Einstein.
  1 Tick the questions it answers from ex.2 above.
  2 Listen again with the Tapescript (*p.110*). Check your answers to questions a to f. Underline more details for each.

4 Look at the phrases. Guess four things about Einstein's personal life. Listen and check.

pregnant	marry	give birth to	have an affair

5 In groups, what do you think?
  1 What's your opinion of Einstein now?
  2 What standards of behaviour do you expect from the people you admire?

When a man sits with a pretty girl for an hour, it seems like a minute. But let him sit on a hot stove for a minute, and it's longer than any hour.
That's relativity.
Albert Einstein

English in use
Giving general impressions

1 Look again at these expressions from [○1].

   1 Give examples for the words in **bold**.

1 He was lazy at **things** he wasn't interested in, ...	things = *school subjects*
2 children were punished for giving the wrong answer and **things like that**	things like that =
3 he was fascinated by the way the compass always pointed north – he was deeply interested in **all that stuff**	all that stuff =
4 but then he had to go to school and learn **things** by rote	things =

   2 [○3] Listen and repeat. Copy the intonation.

Talking about 'things in general'

Use *things / stuff / people* (*like that*), etc. to give a general impression.

- When you can't be specific, or don't want to be.
  *He was lazy at **things** he wasn't interested in.*

- To talk about a group of similar things. We usually add these expressions onto the end of sentences.
  *They were punished for giving the wrong answer and **things like that**.*
  *I'm not really interested in art and **all that stuff** / and **stuff like that**.*

We can also use other general 'group names', e.g. *people / animals / sports / music*, etc.

  She didn't like visiting people she didn't know.
  I'm not keen on small dogs; I like St Bernards and dogs like that.

places
games
people
things
stuff

2 Finish the statements using the words in the box.

  1 I like scientists, and artists, ... *and people like that.*
  2 I hate football, and rugby, ...
  3 I like visiting churches, and art galleries, ...
  4 I'm not really interested in imports and exports, and banking, ...
  5 I like music and clothes, but I haven't got time for pop stars, and models, ...
  6 What I like about Christmas is the family, and food, and presents, ...

3 Tell your partner three things you like and three things you dislike.

4 Which word comes next, *and* or *or*? Explain why.

  1 I've got some really old music: Motown, rock and roll, ... *and* ...
  2 I haven't got any furniture, saucepans, ...
  3 I've got some really nice party clothes: short skirts, silk tops, ...
  4 I haven't got any furs, expensive jewellery, ...
  5 I've still got some of my old toys: trains, a teddy bear, ...
  6 I've got a word processing programme, but I haven't got any games ...

---

and / or

Use general expressions after *and / or* like this:

and + ...	or + ...
stuff (like that)	stuff (like that)
things (like that)	anything (like that)
so on	

---

5 Finish sentences 1 to 6 in ex.4. Use general expressions.

6 Say two or three things you have / haven't got in these categories.

music	clothes	technology	photographs	household stuff
videos	books	ornaments	jewellery	things from your past

Vocabulary
Dependent prepositions

1 Choose the correct ending, **a** or **b**.

1	My brother is **married**	a	a woman called Jenny.
2	My brother **married**	b	**to** a woman called Jenny.
3	He **met**	a	her at a party.
4	He was **introduced**	b	**to** her at a party.
5	He was **very interested**	a	**by** her.
6	He was **fascinated**	b	**in** her.
7	A friend **gave**	a	**to** him.
8	A friend **gave her number**	b	him her number.
9	And he **talked**	a	her a few days later.
10	And he **phoned**	b	**to** her a few days later.
11	A couple of weeks later, he **proposed**	a	her **to** marry him.
12	A couple of weeks later, he **asked**	b	**to** her.
13	They **visited**	a	**to** Rome for their honeymoon.
14	They **went**	b	Rome for their honeymoon.
15	But when they **arrived**	a	**to** their hotel
16	But when they **got**	b	**at** their hotel
17	she **fell in love**	a	**with** one of the waiters
18	she **was attracted**	b	**to** one of the waiters
19	and two days later, she **ran**	a	**away with** him.
20	and two days later, she **went off**	b	**with** him.

2 ⏱ **Against the clock!** Use the phrases in bold from ex.1. Make as many true sentences as you can in five minutes.

Reading
Winning personalities

1 What personal characteristics are necessary to be successful ...?
- as a ... salesman / judge / scientist / teacher
- in your occupation

2 In pairs, read the newspaper article. What was Charles Cornell like ...?
- before the accident
- after the accident

CAR CRASH MADE SALESMAN 'TOO NICE' FOR JOB

By Luke Harding

A 'talented and aggressive' insurance salesman lost his job because a road accident left him with a much nicer personality, the High Court heard yesterday.

Charles Cornell, 31, was a backseat passenger when the driver fell asleep and crashed on the M11 near Theydon Bois in Essex. Cornell suffered head and arm injuries.

His employers told the court that, previously, he had had the 'talent, stamina, capacity for hard work, and aggressiveness which are necessary for a good salesman.' Since the accident, he had become 'a much nicer personality'. But while his family and friends found that he was kinder, less aggressive, more generous, and 'nicer to be around', to his employers he was 'too nice' and had lost the aggression needed for the job.

3 What do you think?
1 What kind of job could Charles Cornell do now?
2 If your personality became the opposite of what it is now, what occupation would you do?

Using *that* clauses

1 Do you agree? Tick or cross the boxes.

1 You can't be both successful and nice. ☐
2 People usually have to choose between professional success and their personal life. ☐
3 There are many different kinds of success – not all of them are professional. ☐
4 In the end, only money and power really matter. ☐
5 It isn't possible to be rich and still have real friends. ☐
6 Your family is the most important thing in life. ☐
7 Every successful person stands on their family's shoulders. ☐
8 Power corrupts and absolute power corrupts absolutely. ☐

2 In pairs, choose three statements. Use these sentence starters to compare your opinions.

I agree that …   OR   I don't agree that …
I think that …   I don't think that …

Expressing opinions

Using *think*

I think …   I think **you can be** both successful and nice, but it's very difficult.

I don't think …   I don't think **you can be** both successful and nice.

We usually use an affirmative sentence after *I think / I don't think* NOT ~~I think you can't be~~ …

Other verbs
I strongly believe (that)   I admit (that) …, but
I can't believe (that)

Adjectives
I'm sure (that)   It's obvious that
It's not true that   It's ridiculous to say that

Nouns
It's a fact that   It's a complete myth that
The idea that … is simply wrong. I don't like the idea that

---

3 🔲 Listen and repeat. Copy the intonation.

4 Say something about opinions 1 to 8 from ex.1. Use phrases from the **Expressing opinions** box.
*I **don't think** it's possible to be rich and still have friends.*

Change pairs. Cover your book. Compare your opinions from memory.

---

that clauses

Reporting sentences contain two clauses.

Comment clause	*that* clause
I don't think	… (that) Einstein was ever lazy.
I was really shocked	… that Einstein was so horrible to his wife.
There's this idea	… that Einstein was a lazy child.

Many verbs, adjectives, and nouns can take a *that* clause.

Verb	I don't **think** (that)
Adjective	I was really **shocked** that
Noun	There's this **idea** that

that is optional with many adjectives and verbs (e.g. *admit / believe / think / be sure / be obvious / decide / promise / realize*).

It's **obvious that**
It's **obvious** | rich people have lots of friends.

 Against the clock!

5 Set a time limit ▨
In pairs, finish all the comments in the box below.
*I **hope that** my English will improve.*

More expressions with *that*

Verbs
My parents always **said** that   I **hope** that
Teachers often **suggested** that

Adjectives
I'm **disappointed** that   I'm **proud** that
Most people are **afraid** that   It's **worrying** that

Nouns
It's an unpleasant **fact** that   It's **a shame** that
There's **a common belief** that

Remember
- Include general expressions like *thing / stuff / people / anything*, etc.
- Use words with their correct dependent prepositions.
- Use expressions with *that*.

Speak out
Talking about people who matter

1 Add two people to the Hall of Heroes. They can be alive or dead, famous or unknown, special to the world or just to you. Think about why you chose them:
- their achievements
- the difference they made to other people
- their personal qualities

2 In groups, describe your two people. Persuade the group to vote for them. Compare how you voted with the class.

15

JOURNEYS

Speaking
Adventure

1 What happens in this article?

2 In pairs, imagine someone calls you and says, 'Meet me in ....' Where would you most like to go? Why?

In April I felt the urge to clear my head among the mountains. From Sydney, I called my wife and told her, firmly, to meet me in Nepal.
'I can't,' Elizabeth said in a dispirited voice. Her favourite aunt was having her ninetieth birthday party in Boston.
'The offer's open,' I said. 'Call me if you change your mind.'
'I've changed it.' *Bruce Chatwin*

Bangkok

Hi Joe — finally got here. Journey awful: flight delayed, service appalling. Then diverted to Vladivostok with engine trouble. Terminal buildings all closed; severe lack of information. Touched down at Bangkok 5 hours late! Then had to wait 40 minutes for them to take us off the plane — at 3.00 a.m! Luckily, hotel's great: be jealous! See you soon, Megan ✕✕

¥ ≤E∅B2≥

J. Fl
49
Chi
Oxc
OX
UK

Vocabulary tip

Learn new words through stories. Most people usually remember stories.

- Link new words together into a story. You can include words not related by topic.
- Learn a group of new words from a story someone tells you.

Vocabulary
Word combinations

1 ⏱ **Against the clock!** In groups, continue these lists for five minutes. Who has the most?

	Places	Things	Events	People
Plane travel	airport	suitcases	you check in	passengers

2 Read Megan's postcard. Where is she? What happened?

3 What travel problems do these words refer to?
1 delayed = *flight*   2 appalling   3 diverted   4 closed   5 lack   6 late

4 Read about Megan's return flight.
1 Complete sentences 1 to 10. Use these words.

down	of	off	on	onto	to

1 We checked _onto_ the flight in good time.
2 But we were delayed due _____ engine trouble.
3 We got _____ the plane two hours late.
4 And we eventually took _____ at 2.00 p.m.: five hours late.
5 But then we were diverted _____ Delhi.
6 There was a severe lack _____ information.
7 When we landed, we all got _____ the plane.
8 They made sure that no one was _____ board ...
9 because _____ the danger of fire.
10 We eventually touched _____ in London seven hours late.

2 Cover the endings of sentences 1 to 10. Explain the problems on the flight.

Listening

Complaining

1 Dean travelled home from Tel Aviv, Israel, to Gatwick, UK. Look at his notes. Say what happened.

2 🔘1 Listen to Dean.

  1 On his notes, tick the events of the journey as you hear them.

  2 Listen again. What are the main things he complains about?

3 Have you experienced travel delays? Describe a trip that you remember well.

- take off 17 hours late/ technical fault
- two hours into flight diverted to Athens/ problems with the engines
- arrive in Athens/left for 30 mins on plane
- crew taken off before passengers
- waited 40 mins in Athens terminal – no information
- passengers refuse to get back on same plane
- now checking onto Peach airline to Gatwick
- total delay 40 hours

English in use

Controlling conversations

1 🔘2 Listen to an extract from the interview. Notice the phrases in **bold**.

Interviewer	[1] **Well**, eventually, Dean, you took off 17 hours late, which is quite a delay, [2] **isn't it?**
Dean	That's right, 17 hours late, and then we were told that we'd have to divert to Athens.
Interviewer	[3] **So** you touched down in Athens. [4] **What happened then?**
Dean	We were then told that we weren't allowed to leave the plane … we were given really no information at all for about 40 minutes.
Interviewer	[5] **Now**, [6] **is it right that** at one point the passengers actually refused to get back on the flight?

2 What jobs do the phrases in **bold** do in the interview? Complete the chart.

Phrase	Job in the interview
isn't it?	asks Dean to say more about something obvious
_____	starts the interview
_____	'picks up' on what Dean is saying
_____	stops Dean talking about one topic and starts a new one
_____	asks an open question
_____	asks if something is true

3 🔘3 Listen and repeat the 'controlling phrases'. Copy the intonation.

4 How well do you know your partner? Ask about these topics. Use 'controlling phrases' from the box.

come from · live/stay at the moment · **work/study** · think of this town/city · likes/dislikes · places you've been to · **family/friends** · do in your spare time

---

Controlling phrases

You can use these phrases to do jobs in conversations.

- Use question tags (*aren't you/ they?*) to encourage someone to tell you a bit more about something you already know.
- Use *Well, … / OK, … / Right, … / Now, …* to start a series of questions, or to start a new topic.
- Use *And / So …?* to pick up on what someone has just said.

Travel broadens the mind.

Don't travel to escape from your problems – they'll still be there when you get back.

Most people travel for a reason but few people know what it is.

Travelling makes you more independent.

Travel is glamorous only in retrospect.

Reading
Journey of discovery

1 Which of these opinions about travel do you agree / disagree with?

2 Complete these phrases.

opinion arranged	up responsibility	~~parents~~ shy	sweating make

1 respect my _parents_   5 travel _____ the coast
2 express an _____   6 _____ a choice
3 an _____ marriage   7 accept _____
4 a _____ girl   8 _____ in the heat

3 Now read about a Hindu girl called Sumita. Decide in pairs ...
   1 What was Sumita like at the beginning? How did she change?
   2 Think of a good title for the story.

My name is Sumita. I was brought up in Bhor, near Bombay. I was taught to respect my parents and to do what I was told. When I was 12, we were sent to Cambridge by my father's computer company. I was made to feel very different from the other children at my school and I became very shy. Everyone seemed to be more independent than I was. I had never expressed an opinion contrary to my mother's or father's. I had never even said 'no' to them – I did not know how to.

But when I was 17, I fell in love with Dave. He was 19 and we talked about getting married. It had always been understood that my marriage would be arranged for me when I finished school at 18, so when Dave and I were found out, my father said that I had to return to Bhor to marry Prakesh Kumar, the man who had been chosen for me.

Dave and I ran away. He had some money and we spent two weeks travelling up the coast from town to town. The weather was hot. We lay sweating on soft beds with the windows wide open. We ate fish and chips, and drank beer. I made choices.

One morning, Dave telephoned his family and he became quiet. The next day, he said we had to go back. We argued. He said he could not accept the responsibility. I had no money of my own so I telephoned my parents and we both returned. My father was angry but polite. 'Do you love Dave?' he asked me. 'No,' I replied. It was the excitement I had loved. My father asked me to return to Bhor and marry Prakesh Kumar. I said no.

4 Look again at the opinions about travel above. Which ones are true for Sumita?

The passive

1 Compare two versions of Sumita's story.
   1 Underline the differences. How many can you find?
   2 Do they change the events of the story?
   3 Do they change your understanding of Sumita and her family?

Version 1

My name is Sumita. I was brought up in Bhor, near Bombay. I was taught to respect my parents and to do what I was told. When I was 12, we were sent to Cambridge by my father's computer company.

It had always been understood that my marriage would be arranged for me when I finished school at 18, so when Dave and I were found out, my father said that I had to return to Bhor to marry Prakesh Kumar, the man who had been chosen for me.

Version 2

My name is Sumita. I grew up in Bhor, near Bombay. I learned to respect my parents and to do what they told me. When I was 12, we moved to Cambridge for my father's work.

My family had always wanted to arrange my marriage for me when I finished school at 18, so when my father found out about Dave and me, he said that I had to return to Bhor to marry Prakesh Kumar, the man they had chosen for me.

2 Do you need to know what caused these events?

1 I was made to feel different from the other children.

2 Dave and I were found out.

3 Prakesh Kumar (was) the man who had been chosen for me.

3 Tick experiences / opinions which are true for you.

1 I've been delayed several times by public transport.

2 I've been robbed in the past.

3 I've been injured and gone to hospital.

4 I was taught really well at school: I found most subjects really interesting.

5 I want to be corrected every time I make a mistake with my English.

6 I was born in a hospital.

7 I'd like my marriage to be arranged by people who care about us.

8 In my family, we always had to do what we were told.

9 I was punished quite a lot as a child because I was very naughty!

10 Women aren't given the same rights and opportunities as men in my country.

4 In 1 to 10 above, highlight the passive phrase. <u>Underline</u> the past participle. Circle the *be* part.
When I was at school, (I was) considered *to be a genius.*

Active v. passive

There are often two ways of describing an experience.

- The active voice describes what you do to the world and to yourself. It suggests that you make a choice.
  I grew up in Bhor. I learned to respect my parents and to do what they told me.

- The passive voice describes what the world does to you. It suggests lack of choice.
  I was brought up in Bhor. I was taught to respect my parents and to do what I was told.

Using the passive

The passive is a way to avoid saying the cause of events, when we don't need to know / want to say. We use it:

- when it is not relevant or when we don't know who did it.
  Our bags were inspected before we went in.

- to be tactful.
  Mistakes have been made.

Recognizing the passive

The passive has two parts.

Verb *be*	Past participle	
I **was**	considered	to be a genius.
My marriage **would be**	arranged	for me.
Have you ever **been**	robbed	in the past?

5 Practise asking with the passive.

1 Make questions from experiences / opinions 1 to 10.
Have you ever been delayed *by public transport?*
Were you taught well *when you were at school?*

2 Ask your questions round the class. Find one person who says 'yes' for each.

6 In pairs, choose two sentences which are true for your partner, and interesting to you. Find out as much as you can about them.

Speak out
Interviews

Remember

- Use a variety of expressions for describing travel.

- Use the passive to describe things that happened to you.

- Try to practise techniques for controlling conversations.

1 What has changed you?

1 Think of an adventure or a journey or an important stage of your life.

2 Remember the main events. Make notes for five minutes.

2 In pairs or groups, talk about your experiences.

1 Take turns to describe. Try not to read from your notes.

2 Ask questions. Find out if people changed. How do they feel about it?

16
HARD TO EXPLAIN

In this Unit

- Practise recognizing and using expressions for speculating, explaining, and disagreeing.
- Look at how we use non-identifying relative clauses for adding comments and explanations.
- Learn vocabulary for describing belief and chance.

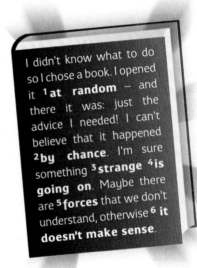

I didn't know what to do so I chose a book. I opened it **¹at random** – and there it was: just the advice I needed! I can't believe that it happened **²by chance**. I'm sure something **³strange ⁴is going on**. Maybe there are **⁵forces** that we don't understand, otherwise **⁶ it doesn't make sense**.

Vocabulary tip

After each stage of a lesson / a conversation / reading an article, write down all the vocabulary you didn't know. Include:
- new words
- new phrases
- word combinations

Challenge!

Remember key words as you go through each section of this Unit. At the end, recall the vocabulary from each section.

Speaking
Dreams

1 The picture shows a scene from a dream. Think of a good explanation for the dream.

2 Do dreams have meanings? Why do you think so?

Vocabulary
Belief and chance

1 Read the text. What is he talking about?

2 Match words / phrases 1 to 6 from the text with the definitions **a** to **f**.

a by coincidence	`2`	d it's impossible to understand ☐
b with no system or method ☐		e mysterious ☐
c is happening ☐		f powers ☐

3 What are the chances of these events happening?

> There's a good chance of it happening.　　It's happened to me.
> It might happen but it's not very likely.　　No chance!
> I've heard of something like this happening.

1 You're thinking of phoning an old friend you haven't spoken to for months. That same day, he / she rings you.

2 You suddenly feel that something terrible has happened. Later, you find out that at exactly the same moment, a close friend had an accident thousands of miles away.

3 You dial a number at random and get through to someone you know.

4 You win £25,000 on the National Lottery just when you need it most.

5 You shout for rain when you need it – and it rains.

6 You're abroad on holiday with your wife / husband / girlfriend / boyfriend, and their previous lover is staying at the same hotel, alone, by chance!

4 Say these words aloud.

accident ●••	happen	power	believe
impossible	random	coincidence	likely
terrible	forces	mysterious	understand

1 Choose the correct stress pattern: ●•　•●　●••　••●　•●••

2 1 Listen, check, and repeat.

Listening
Explanations

1 **[o 2]** Listen. Complete the definitions.

1	*the Guilin Mountains*	a place in _____
2	*residents*	people who _____
3	*yell*	to shout very _____
4	*a pool*	a small area of _____

2 Listen again. Can you explain the strange phenomenon?

3 **[o 3]** Listen to Clare and Andy.

1 What strange event are they arguing about?

2 Who is the sceptic? Who is the believer?

4 Listen again. Who says these? Write Andy (A) or Clare (C).

1 it's not just coincidence   `C`

2 I just don't think that there's anything strange going on   ☐

3 how do they know it was 'at the very same moment'   ☐

4 it could be pure chance   ☐

5 it may be that there's some force that connects people   ☐

6 strange things happen by chance sometimes anyway   ☐

5 In pairs, look at the Tapescript on *p.110*.

1 Summarize a) what Clare believes, b) what Andy believes.

2 Whose point of view do you agree with most? Why?

English in use
Speculating, explaining, disagreeing

1 Clare and Andy use these phrases. Translate them.

It **could be** pure chance …
It **may be** that there's some force that connects people …

2 Practise speculating. How do you think this story originated?
Use the 'speculating' phrases in the box.

> *Two girls who come from the Yunnan province of China are said to be able to make tree branches break and flowers bloom by their 'mental telepathy'.*
>
> Woman magazine

3 **[o 4]** Listen again to Clare and Andy. Complete the gaps.

Andy	_1 Well_____ **I mean**, it is very unusual, but **you** 2_____ I just don't think that there's anything strange going on.
Andy	I 3_____, if we do have these powers, then …
Clare	**I'm not** 4_____ I understand it but it may be that there's some force that connects people …
Andy	**I'm** 5_____ **saying** that it's not very likely.

Speculating

Use *could be / may be* to express possible explanations.

It could / may be …

+ noun	coincidence
+ conjunction	**because** of spirits
+ that …	**that** the air is full of water, and when you shout …

Explaining

Listen out for 'signposting' expressions when someone is explaining something.

- *Well, you see,* and *I mean* show that we are about to explain something (again).

- *I'm (just) saying (that)* or *I'm not saying (that)* show that we are going to say something in a different / clearer way.

4 [5] Listen to how Andy and Clare disagree. Notice the expressions in bold in the **Disagreeing** box.

5 [6] Listen and repeat. Copy the intonation.

6 What do you say to someone who says this?

> I've won £7.50 and £10 on the National Lottery so far. It was raining both times. Obviously, there's a connection. Rain brings good luck to the fields and the plants and so on, so it probably brings good luck to me too. So now I'm only going to play when it's raining and I'm sure I'll win a lot more.

1 Think of three things you could say. Use the expressions from this section.

2 In pairs, roleplay a conversation with this person. Then swap.

SUSPICION

One evening, your girlfriend/ boyfriend ...

Reading
Difficult situations

1 How suspicious are you?

1 Put yourself in this situation. Answer *Yes* or *No* each time.

– rings to say s/he can't meet you.
Are you suspicious?

– says s/he has to have dinner with his /her parents.
Do you believe him/her?

– is seen in a restaurant with someone else.
Are you suspicious?

– isn't at home when you ring at midnight.
Are you suspicious?

– calls you at 12.30 a.m. to say s/he loves you.
Do you believe him/her?

– says the 'someone else' was a cousin: his/her parents were talking to friends at another table.
Do you believe him/her?

– says you can't come round now because s/he has a headache.
Do you believe him / her?

2 Compare in groups. Who is the most suspicious? Who is the most trusting?

2 Look at a true story from a magazine.

1 Where would you expect to find these?

> a fax machine   a phone box   a notice board   an employee number

2 Read 'Wrong number'. Underline the strange events.

3 Cover the text. From memory, explain what was strange.

3 What would Jason say to Helen? What would Helen say to Jason? Roleplay their conversation.

WRONG NUMBER?

When Jason's wife, Helen, saw him in a phone box talking to a woman called Sue, she was suspicious. Would you be? Read what happened.

Sue Hamilton was working alone in her office when the fax machine broke down. Unable to fix it, she decided to call her colleague, Jason Pegler, who had set off home a little earlier. Finding his home number on the notice board, she called him and began to explain the problem. But Jason quickly stopped her. 'I'm not at home', he explained. 'I just happened to be walking past this phone box when it rang, and I answered it!'

The number Sue found on the notice board was not Jason's phone number at all. It was his employee number, which was the same as the number of the phone box he was walking past when she called.

Focus

Non-identifying relative clauses

Non-identifying relative clauses are a way of adding to sentences. They usually begin with *which*, *who*, or *where*.

- They add opinions.
  She thinks it's some kind of mysterious power, **which I think is stupid**.
- They add more detail.
  She called her colleague, Jason, **who had set off home a little earlier**.
  ... a group of pools called the Mysterious Lakes, **where the air is hot and wet**

In everyday speech, they often come at the end of sentences. They are a way of 'adding on' extra bits and pieces as you think of them. In writing, and in organized / prepared speech, they often come in the middle of sentences.

1 Look at 'Wrong number' on *p.66* again.

1 Underline the two non-identifying relative clauses.

2 Complete this version with non-identifying relative clauses.

Sue was working late one evening. There was a problem with the fax machine, _____ , so she decided to ring Jason, who had already gone home. She rang his home number, _____ , and Jason answered it ...

2 These words come from two newspaper articles.

1 What are they about, do you think?

| **A** Jim Fitzgerald of Kilburn, London National Lottery birthplace in Ireland | **B** Loch Ness myth whales and dolphins |

2 In pairs, **A** turn to *p.101*, **B** to *p.104*. Read and memorize your text.

3 Close your books. **A** dictate your text to **B** from memory. Then swap.

4 Now check with the texts. Find four non-identifying relative clauses.

3 In pairs, read these situations. Think of possible explanations. Use a relative clause in each one.

1 After a family meal, everyone is very sick and has to go to hospital – except the person who cooked it.

2 Pedro's waiting for the lift. It arrives, the door opens, and his wife is inside, in the arms of another man.

3 You have just left the office. The security alarm goes off. You go back in to turn it off. The boss is sitting on his desk wearing only his underwear.

4 Which pair has the best explanations?

Speak out
Difficult explanations

1 In pairs, **A** turn to *p.102*, **B** to *p.104*.

Situation 1   **A** is the parent / **B** is the child. Roleplay an explanation.
Situation 2   **A** is the wife / **B** is the husband. Roleplay a coincidence.

2 In situations like this ...

1 Are you more often a sceptic or a believer?

2 Who in the group is the most / least sceptical?

Remember

- Practise vocabulary for expressing belief / disbelief and coincidence.
- Try to include and recognize expressions for speculating, explaining, and disagreeing.
- Use relative clauses accurately for adding comments and explanations.

Vocabulary challenge!	Vocabulary	Listening	English in use	Reading	Grammar	Speak out
Can you remember? In each section, write all the new words, phrases, and word combinations that you can remember from this Unit.	at random	yell	It could be ...	fax machine	myth	jealous

17
WHAT WE WANT

In this Unit

- Talk about how you spend your time, and what you enjoy.
- Look at different uses of *-ing* forms.
- Practise making requests.

Life Enjoyment Profile

very enjoyable

③ +10

②

-10   +10

unnecessary   essential

① -10

not enjoyable

lifestyle: taking control

Part 2: The Happiness Factor

In this, the second of our series on taking control of our lives, we print a selection of readers' answers to the question, 'What makes you happy?'

Readers' Replies

Speaking
Enjoyment

1 Finish this sentence: *Right now, I'd really like to be ...(-ing)*.

2 How much do you enjoy your life? Look at the activities below.

at **home**
doing homework
cooking
sleeping
repairing the car

out and **about**
shopping for food
taking children to school
taking the dog for a walk
going to evening classes

free time
reading
playing football
going for walks
visiting friends

in your **occupation**
working at a computer
writing
having meetings
doing accounts

general life
talking to strangers
talking to family
smoking/drinking
travelling
hurrying/ waiting

1 Cross out the things you **don't do** or **hardly ever** do.

2 In five minutes, for each heading, list all the activities that you **often** do.

3 Now choose the ten activities you spend **most** of your time doing. Put ten dots to represent them on a 'Life enjoyment' chart like this.

4 In pairs, look at your charts. Who has the most enjoyable life, and why?

Reading
Getting what we want

1 In pairs, read the beginning of a magazine feature.
   1 What is the feature about this week?
   2 What answers do you expect from the readers? Make five suggestions.

2 In pairs, **A** turn to *p.102*, **B** to *p.105*. Read the Readers' Replies. Complete the table.

3 Remember the information in the table.
   1 Tell your partner about the Replies you read.
   2 Read your partner's Replies. Do you agree with them? If not, why not?

Using -ing

1 Do you agree with these comments?

1 Cooking is a really relaxing thing to do in the evening.

2 I don't want to have a baby – I couldn't stand the crying.

3 I believe in doing what you want.

4 If you don't like something, avoid doing it.

2 Look at the **Language box** below. Underline examples in comments 1 to 4 above. Then in pairs, make your own comments about cooking, babies, and making decisions.

Four uses of the -ing form

1 As an adjective (usually describing the effect something has on you)
What's the most frightening experience you've had?

2 As the subject or object of a verb
Standing ten feet away from a white rhino is scary.
I don't like visiting people much.

3 After prepositions
Going with someone is very different from travelling on your own.

4 After some verbs, e.g. *avoid, mind, recommend, risk, spend, suggest, believe*
I think you'll be happy if you can avoid arguing.
I spent three days repairing the car.

-ing forms as adjectives and subjects

3 Complete sentences 1 to 8. Use adjectives from the box.

amusing	entertaining	irritating
boring	exciting	terrifying
comforting	exhausting	understanding
confusing	frightening	worrying
embarrassing	frustrating	interesting

1 Everyday activities like cooking and washing are …
… *boring if you do them by yourself.*

2 Monster films like 'Godzilla' are …

3 Learning a new language can be …

4 My girlfriend/boyfriend/wife/husband is …

5 Not having enough money can be …

6 I find work very …

7 Travelling abroad is usually …

8 Visiting people is often …

4 Make sentences with two adjectives you didn't use.

-ing forms after prepositions

5 Match these sentences with **a** or **b**. Explain the difference.

1 I dream of being rich.	a	My husband and me.
2 I dream of **us** being rich.	b	Just me.
3 I worry about driving.	a	I don't like driving.
4 I worry about **him** driving	b	He drives so fast.
5 I often complain about working late.	a	I work late.
6 I often complain about **her** working late.	b	She works late.
7 I'm fed up with smoking.	a	I smoke too much.
8 I'm fed up with **him** smoking.	b	He smokes too much.

6 Finish these sentences so they are true for you. Use an -ing form.

1 I often dream of …

2 I sometimes worry about …

3 I get a lot of pleasure from …

4 I'm bored with …

5 I do sometimes get fed up with …

6 I'm really looking forward to …

7 I think I'm capable of …

-ing forms after verbs

7 Are these good/bad advice for you at the moment?

1 At all times, avoid doing things you don't enjoy.

2 Consider changing your career.

3 You must risk losing some things you enjoy in order to get other things.

4 Spend more time having fun.

5 I recommend prioritizing: decide which things are most important to you.

In English, these verbs are often followed by …
• a noun   *We avoided the discussion.*
• an -ing form   *We avoided talking about it.*

avoid	consider	delay	imagine
keep (on)	mind	recommend	risk
spend	suggest		

---

8 What follows these verbs in your language?

9 In groups, practise giving advice.

1 On your own, write on a piece of paper three things you want from life that you haven't already got. Give the papers to another group.

2 Read the papers and agree on what advice you would give. Use at least two -ing forms.

English in use
Making requests

1 Do the Questionnaire. Compare answers.

2 Imagine you are visiting someone in Britain.
1 What would you say in the situations above? Use *Can/Could I ...?* and *Could you ...?*
2 What answers would you expect?

3 [○ 1] Listen to some requests.
1 How do they pronounce *Can I ...?* and *Could I ...?*
2 Listen again and repeat. Copy the intonation.

4 Imagine you are staying with a British family. Make requests.
• You want someone to phone the station for you to ask about trains to ...
• You don't want to have breakfast anymore.
• You want to understand a strange British custom or phrase (think of one).
• You want to have a friend from home to stay for a weekend.

Making requests

We use *Can I ...?* for smaller requests / with people we know well.

    Can I ... use the phone?

We use *Could I ...* for larger requests / with people we don't know so well.

    Could I ... use your loo?

We use *Could you ...?* when we want the other person to do something.

    Could you ... say that again?

We often give a reason / comment to make our request sound 'softer'.

    Can I use the phone? I have to call a taxi.

We often introduce a request with *I'm sorry, ...*

    I'm sorry, could I use the phone?

Listening
Asking a favour

1 ☼ **Against the clock!** In pairs, skim the extract from a TV magazine in five minutes.
1 What channels are listed?
2 How many fiction programmes are listed, e.g. films, dramas ...?
3 Why is there a number at the end of each programme listing?
4 Find one programme you would like to watch.
5 Find one programme that would be good for your English.

BBC 1

6.35pm Antiques Roadshow
From Highclere Castle in Berkshire, where the experts value a cabinet and an art deco pendant.   261920
7.20pm Holiday Guide to ...
The Holiday Team offer an in-depth guide to the world's top travel destinations. This week, the Caribbean.   885659
8.00pm FILM Chinatown
Thriller set in Thirties L.A. (125 mins, 1974) *Starring: Jack Nicholson, Faye Dunaway, John Huston*   44104

BBC 2

5.55pm Animal Minds
Are dolphins intelligent? The first of a three-part documentary series about the intelligence of animals.   144974
6.45pm Star Trek: Voyager
US sci-fi drama series. Voyager responds to a distress call from an alien ship.   265746
7.30pm The Money Programme
Business and finance magazine.   307
8.00pm A History of Alternative Comedy
Tonight, the new wave of British comedians in the '80s.   7611

Channel 4

8.00pm The Real Albert Einstein
A profile of the famous scientist.   2697
9.00pm Hostage
Second in a three-part documentary series looking at the Beirut hostage crisis. This week, the Iran Contra deal.   1291920
10.15pm Johnny meets Madonna
Johnny Vaughan interviews superstar Madonna.   2720

Channel 5

7.00pm From Jesus to Christ
Last in the series about the rise of Christianity.   5386920
Followed by 5 News Update
8.00pm African Safari
Wildlife series. Tonight, the lion population of Etosha in Namibia. (Rpt)   5362340
9.00pm FILM Bird on a Wire
Comedy thriller (105 mins, 1990) *Starring: Mel Gibson, Goldie Hawn and David Carradine*   972069

SPORT

SKY SPORTS 1
3.00pm Football – Live
Cup Final: Kick-off 4.00pm   7927727
6.30pm Football – Live
Coverage of one of the weekend's matches in Spain's Primera Liga.   80185
8.30pm Unbelievable Sports   5833
9.00pm American Football – Live
Coverage of the second NFL Championship match. 52291

2 Lynn and Mick are visiting friends. Listen to **Part 1**. Number the things Lynn says in order.

- ☐ asks someone to video something
- ☐ asks to look at the TV information
- ☐ asks to use the phone

3 Listen to **Part 2**.
1 Circle the TV programmes which Lynn asks Sean to record.
2 What tape does she ask Sean to use?

4 Listen to the whole thing again. Can you hear these phrases?

1 Can I borrow the phone? 6 Could you do me a favour?
2 Can I phone home? 7 Could you video the Final?
3 Yes, of course. 8 Could you not use the tape that's in there?
4 Sure, go ahead. 9 If you could just find a blank tape …
5 Can I borrow a TV mag? 10 And then, if you could record 'Hostage'?

5 Listen and repeat. Copy the intonation.

6 Choose five phrases to learn. In pairs, **A** turn to *p.102*, **B** to *p.105*. Roleplay telephone conversations. Use the five phrases.

Note

For negative requests we just add *not*. *Could you not …?*

The stress is on **not**.

We tend to use *if you could* … (often with *then/just*) later in a series of requests.

… and then, if you could just …

Vocabulary
do the -ing, go -ing

1 Put these activities into two groups in a chart like this.

cooking swimming walking	Jobs/duties	Free time activities
camping climbing travelling	*cooking*	
sailing washing-up cleaning		
shopping dancing washing		

2 Which group of words can we use after …?
- I'm going to do the …? • I'm going to go …?

3 Right or wrong? Correct the wrong ones.
1 I'd like to go reading in the library but it isn't very comfortable there.
2 I went to watch satellite TV at Pedro's house.
3 I'm going playing music this evening at Mick's house.
4 I went to fish when I was in Cambridge, but there's nowhere to go here.
5 I want to go climbing but there are no facilities here at all.
6 We went footballing and the pitch was awful.
7 I'm going to play tennis tomorrow at the gym.
8 My family goes picnicking in the woods every weekend.

---

do or go

do the -ing is used for jobs/duties.
I offered to do the washing-up.

go -ing is used for…
- free-time outdoor or active activities (*picnicking, dancing*).
We're going sailing this afternoon.
- sports, if the sport is a verb (*to fish, to run, to climb*).
He likes going fishing on Sundays.
BUT if the sport is a noun (*football, tennis, basketball*) we use *play*.
He likes playing tennis.

We don't tend to use *go/do* with 'passive' or indoor activities (*reading, watching TV, playing music*).
I'd like to read …
NOT ~~I'd like to go/do reading~~.

Remember
- Include as many phrases as you can to describe activities in your life at work/at home/in general.
- Use *-ing* forms correctly, especially with *go* and *do*.
- Make requests politely.

Speak out
Improving life for everyone

In groups, think about activities and facilities in your area. How can they be improved? Make a list of suggestions. Choose the best three. Present your ideas to the class. Explain the reason for each.

18 FUTURE NOT GUARANTEED

In this Unit

- Learn words for talking about the future.
- Practise speculating about the future with *going to*, *will*, *might*, *may*, and *if*.
- Use phrases for expressing uncertainty about your plans.

West Sussex ecology group
NEWSLETTER

We must prepare for the future. On a personal level, that's why we go to college, take out insurance, and pay into pension plans. On a national level, that is why we have laws, emergency services, and hospitals. We hope for the best and expect the worst.

But there is now no doubt that we also need to do something on an international level because we are likely to face recession, species extinction, and pollution on a global scale. If we don't change the way we live, there is a good chance that we will wipe out our own civilization.

Vocabulary tip

Learn what comes next.

- a single word, e.g. a noun:
  *I predict **disaster**.*
- a group of words, e.g.:
  - *that* clause: *I predict **that there will be a recession**.*
  - to infinitive: *I expect **to see him**.*
  - prepositional phrase: *We must prepare **for the future**.*

Most words can be followed by more than one form. Check in your dictionary.

Speaking
Predictions

1 In pairs, write four things about you or about the world.

Something that will ...	definitely happen	might happen
unfortunately		
hopefully		

2 Compare with another pair.

Vocabulary
Words for talking about the future

1 Read the newsletter. Underline what you agree / disagree with.

2 What comes next?

1 Choose one word from the box

for to that	1 We're not likely _to_ ... 2 There's no doubt _____ ... 3 There's a good chance _____ ... 4 It's a good idea to prepare _____ ...

2 Choose two or three words from the box.

for to that	5 We hope _____ ... 6 We're sure/certain _____ ... 7 We expect _____ ...

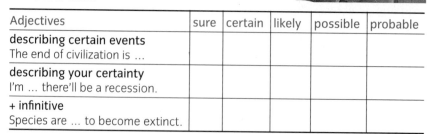

3 How do we use these adjectives?

1 Tick the chart.

Adjectives	sure	certain	likely	possible	probable
describing certain events The end of civilization is ...					
describing your certainty I'm ... there'll be a recession.					
+ infinitive Species are ... to become extinct.					

2 Make the five adjectives negative. Use *un-* or *im-*.

4 Find two places in this sentence to put *definitely / possibly / probably / certainly*.

The world is getting warmer, and we're causing it.

5 What's the possibility of these events affecting you in the future?

losing your way	economic recession	losing your job
pollution	getting ill	the extinction of edible fish
nuclear war	an earthquake	being in a house fire
an asteroid strike	getting old	being in a car accident

I'll **certainly** lose my way at some point.
An earthquake is **unlikely** where I come from.

Listening
Getting information

1 In groups, think of five news stories you've heard recently.

2 Write questions you can ask yourself when you hear a news item.
   1 I/understood / it?   3 /important?   5 How/feel/about it?
   2 /true?   4 How/affect/me?

3 Listen to this item of TV news.
   1 What's it about?
   2 What pictures do you think they showed on the TV?

4 True or false? Listen again and check.
   1 Asteroid XF11 is half a mile in diameter.
   2 It is certain to pass close to the Earth.
   3 There's a one in a thousand chance that it will hit us.
   4 *Deep Impact* is a film by Stephen Spielberg about asteroids hitting the Earth.
   5 If Asteroid XF11 hits us, it could kill a billion people and wipe out civilization.
   6 You're more likely to be killed in a car accident than hit by Asteroid XF11.

5 Answer the five questions in ex. 2. Explain your answers in groups.

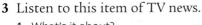

Speculating about the future

1 Look at opinions 1 to 3.
   1 What are they talking about in each text?
   2 Do you agree with them?

2 Look at expressions they use to refer to the future.
   1 Highlight these future forms in the texts.

going to	may/might/could	might well	won't
will	will definitely	will probably	

   2 Put them in the chart below.

- **to suggest absolute certainty / inevitability**
  going to _____ _____ _____
- **to suggest possibility and to speculate**
  ← _____ _____ _____ →
  more possible   less possible

1 You can't be absolutely certain what's going to happen in the future. No one would ever dare to say, 'This is going to happen', or 'This is sure to happen', because there could be a nuclear war tomorrow. We might get hit by an asteroid next week.

2 I think the way we live may change but we won't. I think we will probably stay the same. Some of us may be living on Mars, but we'll still be the same kind of people.

3 There are some things that we can predict with absolute certainty and others that we can't. For example, all of us will die one day. You will definitely be ill or have an accident some time in your life. You might well have a car accident (especially if you are a male driver). And if you smoke, you will get ill, which is why we always ask that question on life insurance policies.

3 Set a time limit

Make as many true sentences as you can from the chart.

I'm going to live until I'm 100.

I I'm	will may / might / could going certain / sure	to … …

4 Now relax. Look at these opinions about smoking. Which sentence do you agree with most? Why?

1 If you smoke, you will get ill.

2 If you smoke, you will probably get ill.

3 If you smoke, you might well get ill.

4 You won't get ill just because of smoking.

5 🔲 Listen and repeat the sentences.

6 Which of these events might happen to you?

- fall in love
- get angry
- get a new job
- pass an exam
- not come to class
- get wet

Use these words and phrases.

I …	will might	won't may	might well could	+	if I

I might go abroad if I get a new job.

7 What's the possibility of these events happening to you? How might they happen?

- get married (again)
- become a millionaire
- have an accident
- live in another country
- lose your way
- catch a cold
- get a medal
- be on TV
- lose all your money
- keep your health well into old age

ARE YOU IMPULSIVE?

How do you make important decisions? Find out with this week's Quick Questionnaire

Which advice do you agree with most? Circle **a** or **b** each time.

1 a If you have a decision to make, take your time: the consequences could last forever.

b Make an instant decision. If you think about things too much, you'll find reasons to do things that you don't really want to do.

2 a Your feelings may change. Make a list of pros and cons and compare them.

b Trust your feelings. Decide with your heart, not your mind.

Reading
Making decisions

1 In pairs, do the Questionnaire. How similar are you?

3 a Deep inside, you know what you really want, so if you have any doubts, don't do it!

b Don't be controlled by your fears. Take a risk! You always regret the things you don't do.

4 a If you are unsure, get someone else's opinion: someone who knows you well.

b Don't let other people persuade you: you are the one who will have to live with the consequences.

5 a If you have two choices, predict what the consequences might be, then choose the one that is most likely to lead to happiness.

b Life is too complicated to predict the consequences of any action. If you have two choices, imagine yourself doing them, and choose the one that makes you feel happiest.

RESULTS

The more **a** answers you have, the more careful and 'cerebral' you are.
The more **b** answers you have, the more impulsive and emotional you are.

2 Compare how you make these decisions.

- deciding which flat or house to move into
- deciding whether to marry someone or not
- deciding whether to have a child or not
- deciding how to vote
- choosing between two jobs
- deciding where to go on holiday

3 In fours, **A** turn to *p.102*, **B** to *p.103*, **C** to *p.105*, and **D** to *p.105*.

1 Read and memorize your e-mail message like this:

- Find six key words in the message and write them down.
- Try to remember the message from the key words.
- Test yourself until you can say the whole message correctly.

2 Say your messages aloud to the group. Decide what's happened / what is happening.

3 What would you advise Monica to do? Why?

English in use
Saying you're uncertain

 1 Listen to Steve asking Daniel out for a drink.
   1 Does Daniel go?
   2 What does Daniel do this evening, and why?
   3 What do you think of the decision he's made?

2 Listen again for these phrases. Is Daniel sure or unsure each time? What about?

1 I'm not sure if I can.	6 Oh, I'm sure I'll find a computer company over there.
2 Oh, I don't think so.	
3 Not sure what time we finish.	7 I hope so.
4 Don't think so.	8 I know it won't be easy.
5 Hope not.	

 3 Listen and repeat. Copy the intonation.

4 Read the **Using sure and know** box.
   1 When do we use a *that* clause? When do we use *if* or a *wh-* word (*what / when*, etc.)?
   2 Say what you are sure about and not sure about.

this evening	the weather	next weekend
your career or job	your English studies	your next holiday

Using *sure* and *know*

Positive

I'm **sure** (that) I'll find a job.
I **know** (that) we'll be happy.

Negative

I'm **not sure** if I can (come out).
I'm **not sure** what time we finish.
I **don't know** if I should.
I **don't know** what to do.

Using *think* and *hope*

Positive	Negative
I **think** so.	I **don't think** so.
I **hope** so.	I **hope** not.

5 Read the **Using think and hope** box.
   1 Which is the odd one out? Why?
   2 Reply using *think* and *hope*.
      1 Are you in love*? I don't think so. I hope not!*
      2 Is it going to rain tomorrow?
      3 Is there a party this weekend?
      4 Shouldn't you be in an exam right now?
      5 Wasn't that you on the TV last night?
      6 Didn't the teacher say she'd take everyone out this evening?

Speak out
Making arrangements

In pairs, practise persuading your partner.
   1 Ask your partner to do something ...
      • this evening / sometime this weekend
      • next week
      • any other time in the future

   2 B has decided to leave. A tries to persuade him / her not to. Choose one of these.
      EITHER   A is B's boss.
      OR   A and B are lovers.
      OR   A is B's teacher.

Remember

• Include as many expressions as you can for certainty, probability, and doubt about the future.
• Use *going to, will, might, may,* and *if* correctly.
• Practise phrases with *sure, think, know,* and *hope*.

19
ALL TALK

In this Unit

- Practise phrases to talk about things you've heard.
- Focus on using *say*, and reported speech.
- Learn how to use *ask, say, tell,* etc.

QUESTIONNAIRE

Family secrets

1 Do you think of yourself as ...?
   a secretive
   b open

2 Do you keep secrets from ...?
   a your parents
   b your brothers/sisters

3 Who are you more honest with ...?
   a your parents
   b your brothers/sisters

4 Have you ever said anything which shocked ...?
   a your parents
   b your brothers/sisters

5 Do you ever tell other people's secrets to ...?
   a your parents
   b your brothers/sisters

6 Do you think you have a good relationship with ...?
   a your parents
   b your brothers/sisters

Speaking
What did you say?

1 In pairs, ask and answer as quickly as you can.
   1 Who was the first person you talked to today? What did you both say?
   2 Who was the last person you spoke to before class? What did you both say?
   3 Can you remember one useful thing that a teacher or parent has told you?
   4 What phrases does the teacher typically say? How many can you think of?
   5 Can you remember a joke?

2 How much did you remember? Compare with the class.

Listening
Listening for gist and attitude

1 Answer the Questionnaire for you. Compare in pairs. Say why.

2 🔊1 Listen to a radio interview with two sisters.
   1 Listen to **Part 1**. Write Liz or Kate.

   _____ is extremely secretive.
   _____ can't keep secrets.

   2 Listen to **Part 2**. What is the connection between these things?

secret	France	boyfriend	tell	parents

   3 Listen to **Part 3**. Finish these statements.
   - Kate decided, later, to tell ...
   - Her mother ...
   - Kate was ...

3 What do you think of Kate and Liz's relationship ...?
   - with each other
   - with their mother

4 Ask in pairs. How similar are you?
   1 What sorts of things do you (and don't you) tell your parents? Why?
   2 Do your parents tell you what they're thinking or how they feel?
   3 Do you pay any attention to the things that they tell you?
   4 Are grandparents important in your family life?
   5 What sort of relationship would you like to have with your children?

Vocabulary
Reporting verbs

answer
ask
explain
promise
say
speak
talk
tell

1 ⏱ **Against the clock!** Which group can finish first?

1 Take turns to explain the meanings of the reporting verbs in the box. The others guess which one you're talking about.

2 One verb from the box goes in all these phrases. Which one?

They _____ me yesterday.

They _____ me to go abroad last week.

Then they _____ me if I had ... (a pen).

2 Correct the use of *ask*, *say*, and *tell* in these sentences.

1 I didn't say my parents anything when I was young.

2 Once I asked to them if I could visit a friend. They told yes.

3 Then my friend and I went off camping. I didn't tell to my parents what we were doing.

4 And I said my friend not to say them anything either.

5 I did say them about it later, and they told that they knew.

6 They asked me that they had followed us and made sure that we were all right.

3 Number Kate's story about her sister Liz in order.

☐ Unfortunately, Liz **told** my parents. But she **asked** them not to **tell** me that she had **told** them.

☐ **1** Terry **asked** me if I'd go to Toulouse with him for the weekend. I **said**, 'Oh, I'd love to.'

☐ So I **asked** her why. And she **told** me that my sister had already **told** her!

☐ I **told** my sister, Liz, what I was doing, but not my parents. Liz **said** that I should tell them.

☐ A few months later, I **told** my mother about it. She wasn't as shocked as I thought she'd be.

4 Think of a family occasion. Can you remember what was said?

• an occasion that shows what sort of family you are

• an occasion that became a family joke or part of family history

• a significant occasion (e.g. when someone left home / an anniversary ...)

Vocabulary tip

As you make a list of words to learn (e.g. from a lesson), list them under the names of the people who used them / in the order they occurred. Go through the conversation in your head, using the words.

Reporting

Direct speech

We usually use *say* in direct speech ...

• when we are reporting conversations.
*I **said**, 'Do you live round here?' and he **said**, 'No', and I **said**, 'But I always see you round here', and he **said**, 'Yes, I work just round the corner'.*

• when the exact words are important.
*What Neil Armstrong actually **said** was, 'That's one small step for man, one giant leap for mankind', but he probably meant to **say**, 'one small step for a man'.*

1 Practise direct speech. Choose from these activities.

Can you remember any quotations?
Tell your partner.
General de Gaulle said '...'

Can you remember anything that your partner has said this lesson?
You said '...'

What mistakes do you both make in English?
Think of some examples.
What should you say instead?
I often say '...' but you should say '...' instead.

Think of a conversation that you have had in the last week.
How much of it can you remember?
She said '...' and then I said '...'

2 Which of these are true for you?

- When I was young, I didn't know that Father Christmas wasn't real.
- I remember a time when I thought that the moon was the size of my hand.
- I found out that you needed money in shops when I was six.

Think of more examples around the class.

3 Match the pictures to sentences 1 to 4.

1 I told them that Jane was in France.
2 I told them that Jane had been to France.
3 I said she was going to have a baby.
4 I said she had a baby.

 Against the clock!

4 Set a time limit

Do **a** and **b** probably mean the same (S) or different (D)?

| D | **1** | **a** | Ann told Joe that she had bought two tickets to Wimbledon for his birthday. |
| | | **b** | Ann told Joe that she was going to buy two tickets to Wimbledon for his birthday. |

| | **2** | **a** | He told her he had taken the day off work. |
| | | **b** | He told her he would take the day off work. |

| | **3** | **a** | His boss said that they were really busy. |
| | | **b** | His boss said that they were going to be really busy. |

| | **4** | **a** | He asked Joe if he would do a few hours' extra work that day. |
| | | **b** | He asked Joe if he had done a few hours' extra work that day. |

| | **5** | **a** | Joe rang work that morning and said that he was sick and wouldn't come in. |
| | | **b** | Joe rang work that morning and said that he had been sick and wouldn't come in. |

| | **6** | **a** | She asked him if he was enjoying the game. |
| | | **b** | She asked him if he had enjoyed the game. |

5 Now relax. In pairs, choose sentences. Tell the story.

| | **7** | **a** | He said it had been the best day of his life. |
| | | **b** | He said it was the best day of his life. |

| | **8** | **a** | At work the next day, his boss asked him if he had enjoyed the game. |
| | | **b** | At work the next day, his boss asked him if he enjoyed the game. |

| | **9** | **a** | He said that he also took the day off – and saw Joe on TV! |
| | | **b** | He said that he had also taken the day off – and had seen Joe on TV! |

Indirect speech

If the speaking was in the past, we usually put the whole sentence in the past (even if it is still true).

A Where's Stuart?

B I think he's gone. He **said he wasn't feeling** very well.

A Oh. That's strange, because he **said he wanted to come**.

Using different tenses

If we are reporting later events or previous events, we usually put the speaking and the events in different tenses.

- If we are reporting plans and intentions, we use *would* or *was / were going to*.
  He **said he would meet** us at 6.00.
  I **told** them I **was going to go** home.

- If we are reporting previous events, we usually use the past perfect.
  He **said he'd been** a singer (when he was younger).

  BUT often, we don't need to use the past perfect if it is already obvious.
  He **said** he **was** a singer **before** he went into teaching.

POP STAR ARRESTED IN CLUB BRAWL

Pop star Bel Hansson (24) was arrested last night when police were called to a club in Soho following a fight in which, it was said, she 'kicked and punched' her partner of two years, the footballer Paolo Rossi (22). Ms Hansson was released after two hours but was not available for comment.

Reading
Comparing and assessing information

1 Read the extract. Explain the highlighted words.

2 Cover the extract. What facts do you know about Bel and Paolo?

3 Now read these comments. Whose side are you on?

Paolo	Bel
having an affair with (someone)	she went wild
carrying on with (someone)	who can blame her?
he dropped her	friends came out in her defence
he had to finish it	she's had a hard time
he was never unfaithful	she just couldn't let go

4 Read more about Bel and Paolo. **Pair A** turn to *p.102*, **Pair B** to *p.105*.

English in use
Saying how reliable information is

1 How many famous names can you put on the board in one minute? They must be alive today.

2 Read the newspaper extracts. Explain these words.

> love nest   dodgy business   love-child   give it up   quarrel   divorce

3 Listen. Which story **don't** they talk about?

4 ☐3 Listen again to the expressions they use. Complete the gaps.

1 I _understand_ that he does have links with the casino business.

2 He _____ me yesterday morning.

3 He _____ , 'I've never really loved her.'

4 I _____ it was Mick Jagger …

5 I can't _____ who told me.

6 But _____ , I don't believe it.

7 _____ , this has been his life's dream.

8 He _____ reporters that he intends to create …

9 Some people _____ it's the Catholic Church.

10 I also _____ that he's been involved with the Christian Scientists.

CAUGHT IN THE ACT! – ██████ and ██████ caught by the camera in 'secret' holiday love-nest.

██████'s name linked with dodgy casino business.

EXPOSED! A love-child for showbiz star ██████ – but who's the father?

'I've seen the light!' – ██████ to give it all up for God.

Family quarrel as ██████ spends entire fortune on art gallery.

'I never really loved you' – bitter words as ██████ and ██████ divorce.

Talking about what you've heard

We use different phrases to show how reliable the information is that we've heard.

- He told me / He said that
  = **this is first-hand information (I know it's true)**

- I understand that / I heard that
  Some people say (that) / Apparently / I can't remember who told me, but …
  = **I got this from someone else**

- Personally I don't believe it / I reckon …
  = **this is just my opinion**

☐4   5 Listen and repeat. Copy the intonation.

6 In pairs, practise gossiping about Bel Hansson and Paolo Rossi. Use phrases from the box above.

Speak out
Start a rumour

1 In groups, think of stories to talk about.

1 Look again at the headlines in English in use. Complete with the names of anyone you like.

2 Think of one more story, about someone famous or someone you know.

2 Talk to everyone in the class. Pass on your information to as many people as you can. Pass on any rumours you hear.

Remember
- Use reporting verbs correctly, especially *ask*, *say*, and *tell*.
- Remember to use the correct tenses in indirect speech.
- Try to include phrases which show where the information comes from.

20
ALL CHANGE

In this Unit
- Use *would* and *could* to discuss suggestions and possiblities.
- Practise making *if / I wish* sentences to describe imaginary situations.
- Build compound nouns.

Vocabulary tip

Plug in to global culture – because most of it is in English.
- watch satellite TV
- buy your favourite English speaking music and translate the song
- log on to the Internet
- get an international magazine or newspaper (e.g. *Guardian Weekly, New Internationalist, Time*)

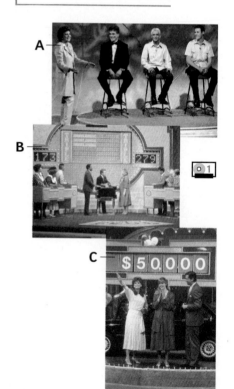

Speaking
Global culture

1 What similarities / differences can you think of between Australia and Canada?

2 Put the countries in the box into cultural groups. Add one more to each group.

the USA	Afghanistan	Ethiopia	Indonesia
Spain	Germany	Brazil	Japan
Sweden	New Zealand	Saudi Arabia	Morocco

3 If you could live in another country for a year, where would you go?

4 Explain the word 'globalization'. Is it positive or negative?

Listening
Listening for opinions

1 Look at the photos.
   1 Which show …?
   is a dating game ☐   is a quiz game ☐   has huge prizes ☐
   2 Explain the following phrases.

   | game shows | celebrities | educational value | consumer interest |

   3 Do you have similar TV shows in your country? Which do you like / dislike?

2 Listen to a programme about game shows around the world.
   1 Listen to **Part 1**. Which shows do they talk about?
   2 Listen again. Tick these opinions when you hear them.
      ☐ Game shows would sell best into 'western cultures'.
      ☐ The world is a lot more diverse than people think.
      ☐ In many places, there isn't the consumer interest for prize shows.
      ☐ Dating games would not do well in religious societies.
      ☐ Quiz shows are thought to have some educational value.

   3 Listen to **Part 2**. Complete the gaps.
      1 In many countries, they like to see _____ on TV, not ordinary people.
      2 In many countries, they don't like people to win _____ prizes.

3 In groups, decide on five TV programmes you would put on a satellite channel. Who in the class would watch your channel?

Vocabulary
Compound nouns

1 Make compound nouns which came up in the radio programme.

game show

game	consumer	quiz		programme	interest	game
dating	prize	television		show	winner	

2 [○2] Listen, check, and repeat.

3 ☀ **Against the clock!** In pairs, make as many compound nouns as you can in three minutes. Be prepared to explain what they mean.

programmes	magazines	news	films	stories	technology
issues	change	food	clothes	events	life

human interest	_____	family	_____	world	_____
health	_____	food	_____	convenience	_____
communications	_____	detective	_____	love	_____
fashion	_____	designer	_____	sports	_____
computer	_____	climate	_____		

4 These are all part of 'global' culture.
1 Where did they originate?
2 How many more can you list in one minute?
3 What is your country's most famous export to the world?

Stress on compound nouns

Most compound nouns are pronounced with only one stress.

game show ● •

There are also three-word and four-word compound nouns.

modern **languages** teacher
multiple **organ** transplant
human interest **television** programme

Note that new words are 'invented' all the time in this way!

Godzilla	Kung Fu	the UN
hamburgers	the Internet	pizza
jeans	the sauna	
satellite TV	whisky	

I would pick more daisies

If I had my life over again
I'd dare to make more mistakes
    next time.
I'd relax.
I'd be sillier than I've been this trip.
I would take fewer things seriously.
I would, perhaps, have more actual
    troubles
but I would have fewer imaginary
    ones.
I would climb more
    mountains, swim
    more rivers.
I would eat more ice
    cream and less
    beans.
I would go to
    more dances,
    and ...
I would pick
    more daisies.

Nadine Stair

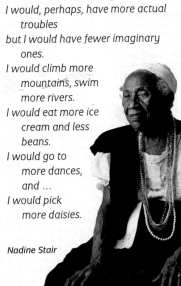

Reading
Making inferences

1 Read the poems quickly. What sort of people wrote them?

If I could change

I'd be free, if I could change
If I could take my past off like handcuffs
And walk into a new life beyond the prison gates
If I could have Dad back, and not fight with Mum
And if no one knew me or knew where I've been
And asked no questions
I'd be free.
So if one night they left the
    doors open, and a new
    suit of clothes,
And a new name, I
    could walk out into
    the night, unseen,
And be free.

Jimmy Tyler

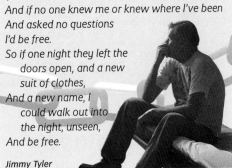

If I ruled the world

If I ruled the world
Everyone would have
    the same amount
    of money,
We would be safe
    in traffic,
No one would go
    hungry
And everyone would
    be happy.
There would be more sport in school
And less crime in the country.
Telephone calls would be free
So that we could always talk to
    each other and be more friendly
And there would be no rubbish in
    the streets.

Sylvie Aerts

2 Describe what the writers are probably like. Include these words.

depressed	serious	sensible	idealistic	naive	confused	worried

3 Complete this description of Sylvie Aerts. Describe Nadine and Jimmy's lives in the same way.

> Sylvie Aerts is at school, obviously. She's worried about _____ , so maybe she lives in a town. She likes _____ . She's more worried about the _____ than about her own life, so she probably has quite a secure life. She's very _____ .

The second conditional

1 Look at sentences **a** to **c**.

These sentences describe …

- situations which aren't real.
- the results if they were real.

a If I had my life over again, I'd dare to make more mistakes next time. I'd relax.

b If I ruled the world, everyone would have the same amount of money.

c I'd be free if I could change. If no one knew where I've been and asked no questions, I'd be free.

1 Underline the unreal situations. Circle the results.

2 What word is 'd in the sentences?

3 Check your answers in the Language box below.

Talking about unreal situations

When we describe an imaginary situation in the present or future, we use a past tense. We also often use *wish* or *if* …

> I wish **I didn't have** so much to do. (= I have got a lot to do and I don't like it.)

When we talk about the results of the imaginary situation, we use *would*.

> **Would you be** any happier with less to do?

> If I could just spend one week getting things organized, **I'd feel** a lot better.

> **I'd be happier** if I had more time to myself.

Remember, we use *could* BOTH as the past of *can* AND to mean *would be able*.

> If I **could** afford it, I'd go to Thailand – and you **could** come with me.

Against the clock!

2 Set a time limit

Look at Anita and Yvonne's 'wish lists'. Describe their lives now.

Anita doesn't have a car. It's difficult for her to get into college.

Anita's wish list	Yvonne's wish list
1 a car – get into college more easily	1 more free time – play with the children more
2 a summer job in TV – help get a job when I finish college	2 an extra room – Bianca's bedroom
3 brilliant tennis player – Ali notice me	3 live closer to parents – babysit
4 more independent – a flat of my own	4 a pay rise – go away on holiday

3 Complete what Anita says to a friend.

1 It _would be_ great to have a car. If I _____ a car I _____ no trouble getting into college, or coming home late.

2 If I _____ a summer job at the TV station, I'm sure it _____ me get a job as a journalist when I finish college.

3 Ali's only interested in tennis. If I _____ a brilliant tennis player, then he _____ me. But I can dream!

4 I wish I _____ more independent. If I _____ a flat of my own, I _____ be with my parents all the time! And then you _____ come and stay with me!

4 Now relax! Write four sentences that Yvonne might say.

5 Finish these sentences. Compare in pairs.

If I didn't have to work / go to college …
If I had more time …
My life would be just that little bit better if …

For Sale Ford Escort; 5 years old; Excellent condition; £2,500 o.n.o. *Phone Leslie 01423-883527*

Bike for sale Yamaha 250: 6 years old; £150 - Bargain! *Call Dave 883494*

English in use
Considering possibilities

1 Listen to Anita and Yvonne talking about these adverts. Do they decide to buy anything?

2 Listen again to Yvonne's suggestions. Write what she actually says.

– a car / Ali / look at it
_____

– a bike
_____

– take lessons
_____

– sell it when you go home
_____

3 Look at this extract again.

1 Underline the imaginary situations.

Anita	**Trouble is**, we couldn't go to the seaside together on it, could we?
Yvonne	Well, I don't know.
Anita	**Plus** it wouldn't be very nice in winter when it's raining and cold.
Yvonne	No.
Anita	**And anyway**, I don't really see myself on a bike.
Yvonne	No, I suppose not. But it would be good fun turning up on a bike.

2 What does Anita use the phrases in **bold** for?

3  Listen and repeat. Copy the intonation.

4 Complete this conversation with *would* (or *'d*) and *could*.

1 A I'd really like to change my job but I don't know what I <u>could</u> do instead.

2 B You _____ go and have a test, to see what you _____ be good at.

3 A I _____ like to write a travel book. Trouble is, I _____ have to give up my job, and how _____ I live without money?

4 B You _____ start by doing it in your free time, _____n't you? Then you _____ get time off work to travel. Where _____ you most like to go?

5 A Peru, I suppose.

6 B Then you _____ go to Peru, take lots of photographs, then you _____ come home and write a book about it!

Speak out
Wish list

1 Tick any of these that you agree with. Think of one or two others.

I'd really like to ...	☐ start my own business.
I want to ...	☐ live in a cottage in the country.
One day I want to ...	☐ get married and have children.
I've always wanted to ...	☐ go to South Africa.
If I could, I'd like to ...	☐ work in television.
Just once, I'd really like to ...	☐ go into space and look down at the Earth.
I wish I could ...	☐ work just three days a week.
I think it would be great to ...	☐ live in a village in Ghana for a year.

2 Write a wish list of up to five wishes. Decide how you would say them using the phrases in **bold** from ex.1 above.

3 In pairs, **A** and **B**, play 'Optimist and pessimist'.

A tell your partner the things you would like to do.

B **You are an optimist** Suggest ways for **A** to do what they want.

A **You are a pessimist** Point out all the problems to B.

Discussing suggestions

We use *would* to talk about the likely results of a situation.

Situation = having a bike
> It **wouldn't** be very nice in winter.
> It**'d** be good fun turning up on a bike.

Situation = going to Brazil
> It **would** be great to go to Brazil.
> I **wouldn't** want to go by myself.
> I **couldn't*** afford it.

(*couldn't here = wouldn't be able to ...)

We use *could* to make suggestions and to talk about possibilities.

> You **could** take lessons.
> You **could** get a month off work.

Remember, *would* is often contracted to *'d*, but *could* is never contracted.

Conditional sentences are often 'shared' between speakers.

Yvonne	If you got a bike ...
Anita	... it **wouldn't** be very nice in winter.

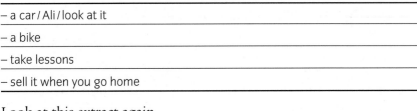

Remember
- Try to use compound nouns.
- Make *if* / *I wish* ... sentences correctly.
- Use *would* and *could* for imaginary situations, and making suggestions.

PRACTICE

01 ALL IN THE MIND

Vocabulary

1 Put these words into three groups. Add two more words to each group.

auxiliary know	learn question	conversation shake hands

Mental activities	Language words	Social activities

2 Write synonyms for:

1 happy _____   4 work friend _____

2 talk _____   5 pay (n.) _____

3 shy _____   6 uncomfortable _____

3 Match six sentences.

1 I was talking   a me feel happy.

2 I explained   b to see her.

3 I said I wanted   c that I loved her.

4 She suggested   d to her one day.

5 She makes   e her often now.

6 I meet   f visiting her.

Questions

4 Make complete questions.

1 (you / think) _Do you think_ (your language / be) _____ easy for foreigners to learn?

2 (it / be / easy) _____ to meet people in your country?

3 (where / young people / go) _____ in the evenings?

4 (how / you / think) _____ (you / can / meet) _____ English people of your age?

5 (why / be / good grammar) _____ important?

6 In your country, (everyone / speak) _____ 'correctly' all the time?

7 (who / not / speak) _____ correctly – and why not?

8 (what / make) _____ a good language learner, (you / think) _____ ?

Starting conversations

5 Complete the conversations.

In the shopping centre

A   [1] _Excuse_ _____ .

B   Yes?

A   [2] _____ _____ _____ _____ where the bus station is?

B   Sure, it's just over there.

A   Oh, hi Pete. [3] _____ _____ _____ for ages. [4] _____ 're things?

C   [5] _____ Jane. Fine. And you?

A   Fine. [6] _____ _____ you've got a new job.

C   Yeah, that's right.

A   [7] _____ 's it going?

C   I'm really enjoying it. And you? What've you [8] _____ _____ to?

A   Nothing much. Same job. Same boyfriend. You know.

02 CHANGING WORLD

Vocabulary

1 Match the beginnings and endings.

1 main   ative

2 mountain   ional

3 relig   ment

4 tradit   ious

5 conserv   land

6 move   ous

7 social   ence

8 citiz   ort

9 influ   en

10 supp   ist

2 Are they nouns, adjectives, or verbs?

3 Put in the missing letter/s.

usi	y	ia	ie	~~is~~	oo	ou	ou	ui

1 _is_ land   4 b ___ ness   7 s ___ stem

2 gr ___ nd fl ___ r   5 famil ___ s   8 offic ___ l

3 b ___ lding   6 c ___ ntry

Present tenses

4 Which sentence describes:

> a changes happening now
> b past events with present results
> c a current state beginning in the past
> d the status quo

1 Life has existed on Earth for 4,000 million years. ☐
2 Asteroids have hit Earth many times in its history. ☐
3 Earth's five continents are still moving apart. ☐
4 One million tons of material from space lands on Earth every day. ☐

5 Translate sentences 1 to 4 in ex.4.

6 Change the verb to complete the sentences.

1 I (live) in Sydney …

   a _I've lived in Sydney_ all my life.

   b _____ because it's so beautiful.

   c _____ while I decide where to go.

2 I (read) 'Secrets' …

   a _____ every summer: it's brilliant.

   b _____ I'm about halfway through.

   c _____ but I didn't enjoy it.

3 Betty (have) …

   a _____ the same boyfriend for ten years.

   b _____ a crisis at the moment.

   c _____ an awful memory.

Being vague

7 Complete this text for your country.

Switzerland is in Europe. It consists of 26 cantons, or regions …

[1]_____ is in [2]_____

It consists of about [3]_____

_____, or regions. Its population

is about [4]_____. There is a big

difference between the [5]_____ and

the [6]_____. The [7]_____

tends to be richer and more densely populated,

and the [8]_____ is poorer. As far

as the climate is concerned, the temperature can

go from [9]_____ in winter up to

[10]_____ in summer. The local food

is [11]_____. In the cities there are

a large number of [12]_____, which

are very popular. It's the kind of place where

[13]_____.

03 LIFE STORY

Vocabulary

1 Make phrases with the verbs below.

get	leave	have	go	move	take

1 _get_____ a job
2 _____ a baby
3 _____ home
4 _____ house
5 _____ married
6 _____ divorced
7 _____ school
8 _____ to college
9 _____ out with s.o.
10 _____ an exam

2 In what order do they usually happen?

Present perfect and simple past

3 Match sentences 1 to 6 with meanings **a** to **f**.

> a finished event (no present connection)
> b a finished period in the past
> c past events in order
> d past event ⟶ present result
> e events in a period up to now
> f a present period which started in the past

1 I've won the lottery: I'm rich! ☐
2 I've had this car for years. ☐
3 I've seen it three times. ☐
4 I got married in 1996. ☐
5 I went to school until 1994. ☐
6 First I had a bath, then I had dinner, then I watched TV. ☐

4 Correct these sentences.

1 Computers ~~had~~ an enormous effect on the world.
   = *have had*
2 I'm only 30 and I was married three times!
3 I'm married since 1995.
4 We've lived there until I've been 16.
5 We lived here for three years now.
6 Elizabeth Blackwell has been the first woman doctor.
7 Have you had a good time last weekend?
8 I've been to the pub and have met some friends, then I've gone dancing till 3.00 am.
9 I'm so happy – look, I won the lottery.

Telling true stories

5 Complete this story about Waris Dirie.

[1] _This_____ is a story of good luck. [2]_____

a girl from Somalia, born in the desert, and she ran away from

her family, [3]_____ to Mogadishu, [4]_____

to London. And [5]_____ she's ended up as a model,

[6]_____ shows what a job in McDonald's can do

for you! ●

6 Make question tags.

1 You were born in Rome, *weren't you?*
2 You married a Frenchman, ...
3 He was a painter, ...
4 You moved to Provence, ...
5 They had two children, ...
6 She lived in America, ...

04 SOMETHING TO DO

Vocabulary

1 How many activities from Unit 4 can you list?

Sport	Leisure	Culture	Other
climbing			

2 Which activities can you use with these phrases?

go ...-ing	go for a ...	go to ...	play ...

go climbing

3 Write the next word or phrase.

1 I really enjoy _____ .
2 I'm not very keen _____ .
3 It's a great way _____ .
4 I go whenever I _____ .
5 I'd really like _____ .
6 I don't really _____ .
7 It's one of my _____ .

Infinitive and gerund

4 Match.

1 I often go ——   a run.
2 Let's   b to run.
3 I'd love   c running.

4 Why don't we   a fly?
5 What about   b to fly?
6 Would you like c flying?

7 She loves   a drive.
8 She'd love   b to drive.
9 She can't   c driving.

10 I'm not keen on a cook.
11 I often like   b to cook.
12 We could   c cooking.

5 Complete the rules.

go + *-ing*	like / love / hate + _____
preposition + _____	would like / love / hate + _____
modal verb + _____	like / love / hate = 'I sometimes
why don't we / let + _____	do it' + _____

Getting information

6 Put one word in each space.

1 I'm thinking *of* _____ coming over _____ Rome.
2 _____ you give me some information _____ museums?
3 I was wondering _____ you could _____ me what the hotels are like.
4 _____ regard _____ sightseeing, could you _____ things to see?
5 _____ hotels, _____ I book in advance?

05 A QUESTION OF LIFESTYLE

Vocabulary

1 Fill in the missing letters. Write the opposites.

a	a	e	ar	e	ea	o	u	or	~~un~~

Opposites

1 *un* fit   *fit* _____
2 ___ wake   _____
3 go to b ___ d   _____
4 lat ___   _____
5 w ___ ke ___ p   _____
6 st ___ t w ___ rk _____
7 h ___ lthy   _____
8 w ___ ried   _____

2 Put these words into a spidergram.

active	have trouble	old people	avoid	diet
sport	stressed	relax	exercise	lazy
cheerful	teenagers	children	guilty	tired

Comparatives

3 Complete the comparatives in the chart.

Regular			
Number of syllables			
short *shorter*		serious _____	
hard _____		active _____	
Spelling			
fit _____	big _____	sad _____	
lazy _____	easy _____	funny _____	
Irregular			
good _____	bad _____	far _____	
Quantity			
much _____	little _____		
Adverbs			
fast _____	hard _____	easily _____	
late _____	soon _____	carefully _____	

4 Complete the rules.

1 One-syllable words take …
2 Longer words usually take …
3 -er words ending consonant / vowel / consonant, double …
4 -er words ending in y, the y changes to …
5 The three irregular comparatives are …
6 Some adjectives and adverbs are the same: they are either -er words or irregular. But -ly adverbs take …

5 Make complete sentences.

1 I'm / tall / my father. *I'm taller than my father.*
2 Pollution / bad / it was 50 years ago.
3 People have / interesting jobs / they did in the past.
4 I work / hard / my parents did at my age.
5 Businesses work / efficiently / they did before computers.

Being indirect

6 Make complete phrases.

1	Not	a	ten a day.
2	It probably	b	of glasses.
3	About	c	quite a lot.
4	It varies	d	really.
5	A couple	e	comes to …

7 Answer these questions using phrases from ex.6.

1 Do you do much exercise?
2 How much do you smoke?
3 How much do you drink?
4 How much do you sleep?

06 CHANGE OF STATE

Vocabulary

1 Move the words in **bold** to the correct sentences.

1 She's the same height ~~from~~ my sister. = *as*
2 She's only 15 – she's **to** young to marry.
3 He's completely different **in** her.
4 They're a good couple: they look **as** similar.
5 They haven't got much **between** common.
6 They're quite similar **very** each other.
7 There are lots of differences **too** them.

2 Make phrases.

1	each	a	like him
2	just	b	height / length
3	hardly	c	other
4	the same	d	ever
5	apartment	a	door
6	move	b	block
7	next	c	country
8	foreign	d	in

Talking about usually in the past

3 Match the past forms with possible meanings **a** to **d**.

1 past simple: *We sang in the church.*
2 would: *We'd sing in the church.*
3 used to: *We used to sing in the church.*

a	once	c	often / regularly / routinely
b	two or three times	d	but we don't any more

4 Complete the gaps using one past form each time.

1 I've changed a lot. I _____ long hair and a beard. I also _____ the guitar and sing folk songs very badly!

2 When I _____ at school I _____ maths because it _____ so difficult. But then I _____ to college and _____ economics.

3 Life was very difficult with Simon. He _____ home and I _____ , 'Let's go out', and he _____ , 'I'm tired', so I _____ out by myself.

Vague expressions

5 Write the missing letters in these vague expressions.

1 ab _o_ _u_ t
2 r _ _ nd ab _ _ t
3 a f _ w
4 n _ _ m _ lly
5 - _ sh
6 m _ st _ f th _ t _ m _
7 a c _ _ pl _ _ f
8 m _ _ nly
9 l _ ts _ f

6 Which expressions can make these sentences 'vague'?

a We have dinner **at eight**. OR *at about eight, …*
b On Fridays, I **always** go out. OR …
c I always see **four** friends on Saturday night. OR …

07 TAKING CHANCES

Vocabulary

1 Read 1 to 8. Make sentences with **a** to **h**.

He was …			
	a terrified.	e	so embarrassed.
	b terrifying.	f	so embarrassing.
	c so bored.	g	very relaxing.
	d so boring.	h	very relaxed.

1 He was happy lying in the warm sunshine by the pool. [h]
2 His gentle voice calmed me. ☐
3 His parachute didn't open. ☐
4 The robber had a gun. ☐
5 He didn't stop talking about it. ☐
6 He didn't understand one word of the whole lecture. ☐
7 But it was the women's showers! ☐
8 He got completely drunk. ☐

2 Find the opposites.

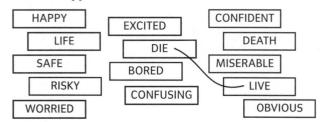

Linking

3 Correct the mistakes.

1 People need adventure ~~because of~~ life is too safe these days. = *because*

2 People live longer because better housing and diet.

3 Most accidents are due carelessness.

4 People are not happy despite of having more money.

5 People are no happier in spite of they have safer lives.

6 Even there are advantages to a technological society, people need more from life.

Finding agreement

4 Write 'Yes' or 'No' to agree with these statements.

1 That's not right. _No._

2 That's OK. _____

3 We can't turn left here, can we? _____

4 We can turn left here, can't we? _____

5 In that situation, there's no time to think. _____

6 I don't think you've met Hari. _____

7 It's not far, is it? _____

5 Complete the replies.

yes/dangerous	nor do	no/hard	yes/same	so do

1 'I enjoy a bit of danger.' '_____ _____ I.'

2 'I don't like many team games.' '_____ _____ I.'

3 'Climbing can be very risky.' '_____, really _____.'

4 'Hang-gliding is the only way to spend a weekend.'
'_____, I feel the _____ about scuba diving.'

5 'Parachuting isn't easy.' '_____ , it's really _____ .'

08 GETTING THROUGH?

Vocabulary

1 Cross out the wrong item.

1 Can I speak to/~~x~~ Maria?

2 I have to call/phone/speak/ring someone.

3 Can I make/do a phone call?

4 You make/have a chat.

5 Can you get/answer/reply the phone, please?

6 Give me a ring/call/phone.

7 Who's it/calling/this?

2 Complete the crossword.

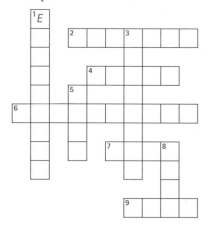

If you know the _1_ number you require, please _8_ it now.

If you need _6_ from the _3_ , please _4_ zero.

Can you _7_ please?

Hello, you're _2_ to the operator, can I _9_ you?

Yes, I'm trying to _5_ someone in Italy.

Future arrangements

3 True or false?

1 *I'm meeting John/I'm going to meet John* = I already have an arrangement with John.

2 *What are you doing this evening?/What are you going to do this evening?* = What arrangements have you got this evening?

3 *Shall I meet you at seven?* = a suggestion. You can answer *How about seven-thirty?*

4 *I'll be there at seven* = you might be there.

5 *I'm about to have dinner* = in the next two or three minutes.

Guiding a phone call

4 Complete three exchanges.

1 A (*picks up the phone*) _Hello_ .
   B Hi, Peter, _____ Simona.

2 C So we'll meet (*you can't hear what he says*).
   D _____ ?
   C We'll meet at the White Swan pub in town.
   D Oh, yes, fine.
   C _____ right then, see you later.

3 E Anyway, _____ you later then.
   F Yeah, _____ .
   E _____ .

5 How many ways of saying 'Yes' and 'No' can you remember?

09 INCIDENTS AND ACCIDENTS

Vocabulary

1 Write the words in the diagram.

lose	divorced	an accident	married
fail	a party	~~pass~~	win

	😊	🙁
exam	_pass_	
competition		
you have		
you get		

2 Match formal and informal phrases.

Formal		Informal
1 my house		a I'll pick you up
2 enjoy yourself		b have a good time
3 I'll collect you		c can't stand
4 formal		d turn up
5 hate		e my place
6 arrive		f posh

Planning the future

3 Complete the answers.

1 Have you got anything planned for this evening?
   Yes, I _'m meeting_ Patrick at 8.30.

2 Why's that lady so fat, Mum?
   She _____ a baby.

3 Do you have any ambitions?
   Yes, I _____ around the world one day.

4 Can you come on Saturday?
   Oh yes, I _____ , don't you worry!

5 I don't know what to get for Jim's birthday. I know!
   I _____ Kate – she _____ what
   to get him.

6 Shall we go to the beach tomorrow?
   I don't think the weather _____ very nice.

7 My plane _____ at 10.00 tomorrow.

4 Tick the columns for the forms we use.

Types of future	Present continuous	_going to_	_will / won't_
it's already arranged			
I know from present evidence			
I intend to do this			
promises / guarantees / offers / requests			
sudden decisions			
uncertainty: hopes / fears / possibilities with _think / probably_			

5 When do we use the present simple to express the future?

Phrases for special occasions

6 Complete the crossword. Find the mystery word.

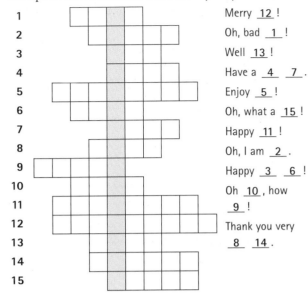

Merry __12__ !

Oh, bad __1__ !

Well __13__ !

Have a __4__ __7__ .

Enjoy __5__ !

Oh, what a __15__ !

Happy __11__ !

Oh, I am __2__ .

Happy __3__ __6__ !

Oh __10__ , how __9__ !

Thank you very __8__ __14__ .

10 OTHER HOUSES …

Vocabulary

1 Complete with a form of _watch TV_. Add _us_ if necessary.

1 We mustn't _watch TV_.
2 They don't let …
3 We're never allowed …
4 They spend all their time …
5 They never stop …

2 Write in the vowels (a e i o u).

m_e_ _a_l t_m_s	th_ w_sh_ng _p
p_dd_ng	th_ m_ _n c_ _rs _

_rg_m_nts	_rg_ _	b_n
g_t _ps_t	_nt_rr_pt	t_lk_ng

3 Think of a title for the two word groups in ex.2.

Obligation and permission

4 Correct the mistakes.

1 In my country, we can ~~to~~ drive at seventeen.
   = _we can drive_

2 In my country, children under sixteen haven't to smoke.

3 In Finland, parents must to talk to their children about family decisions.

4 We don't can get married until we're seventeen.

5 Parents don't have to let their children drink alcohol in pubs.

6 It's allowed smoking in nearly all restaurants in Italy.

7 Ignorance is no excuse – people should to know the law.

8 In my country, you mustn't vote if you don't want to – it's completely voluntary.

Sentence patterns

5 Number the sentences in order, 1 to 4.

- ☐ and find the smell of smoke in the house annoying
- ☐ if you want to smoke
- ☐ because people don't like you smoking indoors
- ☐ it's normal to go outside

6 Complete the gaps.

> **In the lunch hour,** most people go into the town centre, ¹ *because* it's very close, and ²_____, you spend the whole day in the office ³_____ it's much nicer to get out. ⁴_____ there is a canteen ⁵_____ you prefer.

11 TEMPER AND TEARS

Vocabulary

1 How many words match? Write all the letters for each.

1	lose	*c,*_____	
2	feel	_____	
3	get	_____	
4	stay	_____	
5	am / is / are	_____	

- a irritated
- b angry
- c your temper
- d control
- e fed up
- f calm
- g sad

2 Write the noun of these words.

angry	→ *anger*
weak	→
lose	→
sad	→
lucky	→
happy	→
brave	→
enthusiastic	→

Narrative tenses

3 Which tense? Write 1, 2, or 3.

☐ past simple   ☐ past perfect   ☐ past continuous

1 It _____ so I was wet through when I arrived at work but I was so happy that I _____ like a bird.

2 The boss asked me why I _____ late and _____ me into his office. We _____ and _____ .

3 And I told him that I _____ the lottery and that I _____ to leave.

4 Complete 1 to 3 above with these verbs.

> be   decide   rain   sing   sit   take   talk   win

5 Find a sentence from ex.3 which describes ...

1 earlier events

2 being 'in the middle' of one activity when another one happened

3 events happening one after another

4 events of the same length happening together

Complaining

6 Complete the conversation.

I'd like to	but	~~Excuse me~~	I'm afraid
I'd like a	thank you	I appreciate that	please

In the self-service restaurant

A ¹ *Excuse me* _____ .

B Yes?

A ²_____ this meal isn't very nice.

B Would you like another one?

A No ³_____ . ⁴_____ refund.

B I'm sorry, we don't give refunds.

A ⁵_____ , ⁶_____ I still want a refund. ⁷_____ see the manager, ⁸_____ .

12 SAYING NO

Vocabulary

1 Write the base words. Add letters if necessary. List the affixes in the box.

a	useful	*use*	*-ful*
b	straighten	_____	_____
c	sensitivity	_____	_____
d	invitation	_____	_____
e	arrangement	_____	_____
f	significance	_____	_____
g	impolite	_____	_____
h	unhappiness	_____	_____

2 Use the affixes to make new words from these.

1	friendly	_____	5 explain	_____
2	move	_____	6 possible	_____
3	beauty	_____	7 sweet	_____
4	important	_____		

Using infinitives

3 Finish each sentence so it means the same as the sentence before it.

1 I said, 'Please tell me.'   **I asked him** *to tell me.*

2 I didn't tell him because I forgot.   **I forgot** ...

3 It's important that I tell you.   **I have** ...

4 I ought to go home.   **I really must** ...

5 I'm so busy that I can't do it. **I'm too busy ...**

6 I'll wait if you like. **Do you want me ...**

7 Don't change it: there's not enough time. **There isn't enough time ...**

8 Is saying no difficult? **Do you find it hard ...**

9 Should I tell Jane or Frank? **I don't know who ...**

10 I went to the bank for some money. **I went to the bank to ...**

Invitations and replies

4 Complete these invitations and replies.

1 A / fancy / drink?

Do you fancy _____

B Sorry / love to / but / afraid / got to get back.

_____

2 C We (have) a party / Saturday / wondering / like / come.

_____

D / very nice / you.

_____

13 BRAINPOWER

Vocabulary

1 Among these words and phrases, find ...

1 one pair with similar meanings

_____ _____

2 one pair of opposites

_____ _____

3 two that often go together

_____ _____

4 three from the topic 'computers'

_____ _____ _____

disk
major
all the time
erase
event
forget
file
remember
constant

2 Match eight phrases.

1	short term	a	of 3,000 words
2	brain	b	average
3	a few	c	cells
4	a vocabulary	d	ages of 2 and 4
5	between the	e	go
6	on	f	seconds
7	learners	g	memory
8	in one	h	of a foreign language

Defining relative clauses

3 How many phrases match? Write **a**, **b**, and **c**.

1 This is the letter ...   *a,*____

2 This is the person ...   _____

3 That was the occasion ... _____

a that changed her life.
b who changed her life.
c which changed her life.

4 Bracket ( ) *who* or *that* where it isn't necessary.
You always remember ...

1 the major events that happen in your life.

2 the things that you see or use every day.

3 the people who you're close to.

4 the people who are important to you.

5 Make relative clauses. Use *you* if necessary. Then do it.
Close your eyes and describe ...

1 a place / know well   *a place (that) you know well*

2 a person / has helped you _____

3 an object / use every day _____

4 an animal / liked as a child _____

5 someone / admire   _____

6 a song / brings back memories _____

7 a book / changed you   _____

8 a person / makes you laugh _____

Repair strategies

6 What can you do in a conversation if ...

– you can't hear / understand what someone has said?

_____

– you're not sure of the right word / phrase?

_____

– you use the wrong word / phrase by mistake?

_____

– you have trouble forming a sentence?

_____

14 GIVING IMPRESSIONS

Vocabulary

1 What comes next: **a**, **b**, or **a/b**?

1	I'm married	b
2	It was in June that I married	
3	At a party, I was introduced	
4	I loved talking	
5	I fell in love with	
6	The next day, I phoned	
7	In the evening I visited	
8	I gave a ring	
9	I proposed	

a Michael
b to Michael

2 Write the next word. Finish the sentences.

1 He's interested *in*____ ...

2 I'm fascinated _____ ...

3 I was lazy _____ maths but I was quite good _____ ...

4 Last weekend I went _____ ...

5 He was very attracted _____ ...

6 You should give flowers _____ ...

Using *that* clauses

3 Make complete sentences with this phrase.

'success is mostly luck'

1 realize   *I've realized that success is mostly luck.*

2 believe   _____

3 ridiculous to say   _____

4 not true   _____

5 not think   _____

6 afraid   _____

7 this idea   _____

8 obvious   _____

4 Make complete sentences.

1 Jana agreed / I should do it. *Jana agreed that I should do it.*

2 Petra decided / it / too late.

3 Alessandro promised / would ask me.

4 Sung realized / it / important.

5 Ricardo / not / think / it / important.

Giving general impressions

5 Complete the sentences. Include these words.

stuff	anything	things	places	~~activities~~

1 I enjoy tennis, swimming, *and activities like that.*

2 I like busy streets, markets ...

3 I like reggae, salsa ...

4 I haven't got a pension or any investments ...

5 I'm interested in music, poetry, drama ...

6 Write the last word.

1 It's important to know about engines, computers, and so _____ .

2 I hate business, money, banking, and all that _____ .

3 I haven't got a calculator or computer or anything like _____ .

15 JOURNEYS

Vocabulary

1 Complete the puzzle.

1		o			
2		o		o	
3		o			
4		o			
5		o			
6		o			
7		o			
8		o			
9		o			

We eventually got **1** the plane. We checked **2** the flight late. There was a real lack **3** space on the plane. The flight was delayed due **4** snow. Too many people had got **5** board. Half way into the flight, we were diverted **6** Kazan. We couldn't land because **7** the bad weather. But we eventually touched **8** in Moscow. We got **9** the plane exhausted.

The passive

2 Correct the mistakes.

We were spies but [1] *we were employed* (we employed) as diplomats in the Embassy. The international situation was getting worse all the time and on Friday 27th we [2] _____ (were realized) we had to leave the country. We had to avoid [3] _____ (catching) or we would be shot. We [4] _____ (were stopping) three times on our way to the airport by army patrols. I can remember that I [5] _____ (was being shaken) with fear. At the airport, we [6] _____ (were questioning) for fifteen minutes before our interrogators [7] _____ (have called) away. They told us to wait until they [8] _____ (were come back) but we could see our plane through the window ...

3 Look at the text again. Translate phrases 1 to 8. Compare the use of the passive with your language.

Controlling conversations

4 Complete the interview.

And	aren't you?	didn't you?	And is it right that
And is it	~~So~~	Well	Right, now

A ... and we decided to run for it.

B [1] *So* _____ you didn't stay in the room?

A Oh no. We got through the window, jumped on the plane and escaped.

B [2] _____ you left the service soon after, [3] _____

A Yes. Six, seven months later.

B [4] _____ you left because of your experiences?

A No, not really. For other reasons.

B I see. [5] _____ that's fascinating. [6] _____ , um, you're currently writing a book, [7] _____

A Yes, that's right.

B [8] _____ about your experiences as a spy?

16 HARD TO EXPLAIN

Vocabulary

1 Complete the crossword.

Across

1 I knew that he'd had a terrible _____ .

5 Something strange is _____ and I can't explain it.

6 Something is definitely _____ on.

11 There are _____ forces in the universe which influence our lives.

Down

2 We weren't expecting to meet – it was a complete _____.

3 It couldn't happen! _____ chance!'

4 We didn't plan it: it happened by _____.

7 Some people have unusual _____ that science can't explain.

8 I opened the book at _____.

9 It doesn't make any _____.

10 I felt sick at exactly the _____ moment!

Non-identifying relative clauses

2 Add the extra information to this story using clauses with *who* or *which*.

> I was going on holiday to Italy (**1** *which I do every summer*), and I was at the airport in the queue waiting to board my flight when I suddenly felt really worried about my Mum (**2**). I didn't understand it but it suddenly felt like the most important thing in the world (**3**). So I got out of the queue (**4**) and found a public telephone (**5**) and dialled the number. Mum said 'Hello' and was surprised to hear me. She was fine: nothing had happened. But I missed my flight (**6**). I drove home listening to the radio. Thirty minutes later, they said that my plane had crashed, killing everyone on board (**7**).

1	~~do every summer~~	**5**	took ages
2	a bit ill at home	**6**	made me absolutely furious!
3	very unusual for me	**7**	gave / such a shock / had to
4	thought / really stupid!		stop the car

Speculating, explaining, disagreeing

3 Complete the conversation.

Look	sorry	it could be
but	I'm not saying	I just don't see
Well	I mean	~~can't be~~

A Something like that ¹ *can't be* coincidence.

B Why not?

A ² _____ it's just too much of a coincidence, isn't it? ³ _____ , that sort of thing can't happen by coincidence. ⁴ _____ , ⁵ _____ it's impossible, but it's very unlikely. There's got to be a real connection.

B What, like time going backwards – the plane crashes so he misses the flight?

A No, something simpler, I mean ⁶ _____ intuition ...

B Well, no. I'm ⁷ _____ ⁸ _____ I can't believe in intuition. ⁹ _____ how you can believe that.

17 WHAT WE WANT

Vocabulary

1 Choose the best form (**a**, **b**, **c**, or **d**) each time.

> **a** do the ...-ing (I did the shopping)
> **b** go ...-ing (I went shopping)
> **c** – (I shopped)
> **d** play + sport (I played handball)

1	I can't come yet: I've got to (wash up).	a
2	I (sail) yesterday.	
3	It's the secretary's job to (file).	
4	Last Saturday we all (tennis).	
5	I bought a good book and (read) all day.	
6	Last winter, we (ski) in the mountains.	
7	Does anyone want to (listen) to some music?	
8	Did you (dance) yesterday?	
9	Has anyone offered to (clear up)?	

Using -ing

2 How do you say these in your language?

1 It was a fascinating film.
2 The acting was good but I didn't like the singing.
3 I'm tired of working here.
4 I can't imagine having lots of money.

3 Rewrite these sentences using an *-ing* form.

1 I said, why not buy a car? **I suggested** *buying a car.*
2 I think I might go to India. **I'm thinking of** ...
3 Don't get caught in the traffic. **Try to avoid** ...
4 Is it possible to swim there? **Is there any chance of** ...
5 Why not buy one? **Have you considered** ...
6 She really annoys me. **She's** ...
7 I'd quite like to see the city. **I'm interested in** ...
8 I planned it for ages. **I spent ages** ...
9 That place is full of excitement. **It's** ...
10 It's not good to shout at children. **I don't believe in** ...
11 All the time, I thought, 'There's no one here.' **I kept** ...
12 The house is difficult to find. **The problem is** ...

Making requests

4 Match.

1	Can I	a	get me a drink?
2	Could you	b	have a drink?
3	Could I	a	borrow it?
4	Could you	b	say that again?
5	Could I	a	smoke in here?
6	Could you not	b	make so much noise?

5 Complete the conversations.

A I'm ¹ _sorry_ , ² _____ I just close the window? ³ _____
feeling ⁴ _____ cold.

B Sure. Go ⁵ _____ .

C ⁶ _____ you help me move this sofa, please?

D Yes, of ⁷ _____ .

C Thanks, and ⁸ _____ we could ⁹ _____ put it over there ...
And could you ¹⁰ _____ put it on my FOOT!

D Sorry!

18 FUTURE NOT GUARANTEED

Vocabulary

1 Put the words in order.

1 definitely get I'll think promotion I

2 probably the miss will us asteroid

3 going is the party Helen certainly to

2 Which words can go next? Write the letters.

1 A disaster is _a,_ _____ .

2 Are you _____ ?

3 Yes, it's _____ to happen.

a sure	d certain
b possible	e probable
c likely	

3 Write the next word(s).

1 We're unlikely _to_ ...

2 There's no doubt _____ ...

3 There's a good chance _____ ...

4 We should prepare _____ / _____ ...

5 I'm sure _____ / _____ ...

6 I expect _____ / _____ ...

4 Finish sentences 1 to 6 so they are true for you.

Speculating about the future

5 Which words are followed by *to*?

1 will / won't [✗] 3 could [ ] 5 be certain [ ]

2 may / might [ ] 4 be going [ ] 6 be sure [ ]

6 Write the missing letters.

I've applied for a new job. I'm well qualified for it, so ...

1 I'll _ _ o _ a _ _ y get an interview,

2 I might _ e _ _ get the job, but even if I don't,

3 I'll _ e _ i _ i _ el _ know by the end of the month.

7 Make sentences.

1 Some things are certain. For example, all of us
will die one day.

2 Summer _____ be warmer next year than this
year, or maybe not – who knows?

3 I love being really hungry and knowing I _____
eat soon.

4 I'm sure you _____ have any trouble at the
airport. It's always really quick.

5 I'm _____ get stopped at customs: I always do.

6 I think Dana's in town at the moment: if you
_____ to the party tonight, you _____
meet her – you never know!

7 If there _____ a war, I don't know what we
_____ .

Saying you're uncertain

8 Complete the gaps.

I'd like to meet him at the station but ...

1 I don't know _what_ _____ his train arrives.

2 I don't know _____ train he'll be on.

3 I'm not even sure _____ he's coming today.

4 And I'm not sure _____ his telephone number is.

9 Tick the possible replies.

Does he love you?

1 I think so. [✓] 4 I don't hope so. [ ]

2 I hope so. [ ] 5 I hope not. [ ]

3 I don't think so. [ ]

19 ALL TALK

Vocabulary

1 Write *asked*, *said*, *talked*, or *told*.

1 I _____ that I played jazz.

2 I _____ (to her) about jazz.

3 I _____ (her) about jazz. / (her) if she liked jazz.

4 I _____ her about jazz.

2 Complete each question with *say, ask, tell,* or *talk*.

1 How long did you _____ for?

2 What did you _____ about?

3 What did she _____ ?

4 Did she _____ you if you're married?

5 Did you _____ her we're married?

6 Did you _____ her about her plans for the weekend?

3 Match with **a** to **f**.

1 She talked (to me)	[c]
2 She told me	[ ][ ][ ][ ]
3 She said	[ ][ ][ ]
4 She asked (me)	[ ][ ][ ][ ]

a 'I'm from Mali.'

b (that) she comes
from Mali.

c about world music.

d what 'Salsa' is, and
where it comes from.

e if I had my guitar with me.

f to play something.

Reporting

4 Here is some information about Karin.

> **a** 1990 – 95 maths teacher **b** 1995 – now TV producer

When did she say these? Write **a** or **b**.

1 She said, 'I teach maths'.   [a]
2 She said she taught maths.   ☐
3 She said she'd taught maths.   ☐
4 She said she wasn't enjoying teaching.   ☐
5 She said she hadn't enjoyed teaching.   ☐
6 She said she was going to become a TV producer.   ☐

5 Make sentences about Marcello. Change the verb form if necessary.

> **a** 1984 – 97 musician **b** 1998 – now politician

1 1985   He said, 'I / musician'.
2 1986   He said he / musician.
3 1996   He said he / go into politics.
4 1997   He said he / try to change jobs.
5 1997   He said he / give a final performance in Rome.
6 1998   He said, 'I / musician'.
7 1999   He said he / enjoy life as a musician.
8 1999   He said he / always want to be a politician.

Saying how reliable information is

6 Complete the crossword.

PIA MONTE QUITS NEW BOND FILM

So, why has the film star Pia Monte walked out of the new Bond film? I h _7_ that she needs the money and a _8_ she is selling two of her houses. But Pia t _9_ m _5_ she left because she doesn't want to do it. Her agent, on the other hand, s _4_ that she's tired and needs a rest. A mystery! I now u _2_ that she doesn't want to talk about it any more. Some p _3_ s _6_ she's ill. But p _1_ I think she's just had another argument with the director. ■

20 ALL CHANGE

Vocabulary

1 Make as many compound nouns as you can.

1 computer	5 designer	change	clothes
2 quiz	6 world	food	music
3 love	7 climate	problem	programme
4 health	8 fast	show	story

The second conditional

2 Put the verbs in the right spaces.

'd get / got could / could	'd be / ~~were~~ 'd have / had	'd have / had

1 If I _were_ rich, I _____ happier.
2 I _____ no trouble getting to work if I _____ a car.
3 I _____ more interests if I _____ more time.
4 If I _____ tired of my job, I _____ another one!
5 I _____ talk to her if I _____ only speak Italian!

3 Answer the questions.
Talking about unreal situations
1 When do we use the past tense?
2 When do we use *would*?
3 When do we use *could*?

4 Complete these sentences.

1 Where I live it _'s_____ quiet, wet, and cold. I wish I _____ in Spain or Greece. (be / live)
2 I'm sure my brother _____ me if he _____ a new girlfriend. (tell / have)
3 I hate being poor. If I _____ a better job, we _____ all right. (have / be)
4 If I _____ to bed earlier, I _____ better in the morning, but I always _____ up in the evenings! (go / feel / wake)
5 In 1922, when Alexander Bell _____, all the telephones in North America _____ silent for one minute. There _____ a disaster if anything like that _____ today. The world financial system _____. (die / go / be / happen / collapse)
6 If there _____ a nuclear war now, there _____ no warning. (be / be)

Considering possibilities

5 Complete this conversation.

A I wish I _1 had_ another qualification.
B What _2_____ you like to do?
A Computing, I think.
B Oh yes, that _3_____ great. You _4_____ able to get another job then.
A Well, yes, I hope so.
B Well why not? You _5_____ do a course.
A Trouble is, I _6_____ afford to take that long off work.
B Well, you _7_____ go to evening classes.
A If I _8_____ the time I _9_____ .
B It _10_ take too much time, only twelve weeks or so. Denise did a course like that. She's earning 30,000 now.

WRITING

01 An introductory letter

1 Complete this letter with words from the box.

boyfriend	studying law	speaking	25 years
never	single	big flat	town
south of	two years	letters	in an office
grammar	pronunciation and vocabulary		

64 Cromwell Road
Littlehampton
BN12 4QT

6 Feb 2000

Dear Anna,

Thanks for your letter and for telling me about yourself. I'd like to tell you something about me.
I'm <u>1   </u> old. I live in a small <u>2   </u> in the <u>3   </u> England. I work <u>4   </u> during the day, and in the evenings I'm <u>5   </u>. I'm <u>6   </u> but I have a <u>7   </u> called Alan.
I live in a <u>8   </u> in the centre of town.
I have <u>9   </u> studied Italian before, but I lived in Italy for <u>10   </u> when I was a teenager. My <u>11   </u> are OK but my <u>12   </u> is awful!
I'd like to practise <u>13   </u> and writing <u>14   </u>.
Best wishes,

Vicky

2 Write an introductory letter to your teacher (150 words).

02 A fact file

Write a Fact File about your country (200 words).

- Look at ...   the Afghanistan Fact File (*p.9*)
  the information about Hong Kong (*p.11*)
- Write information under the following headings:

FACT FILE	
GEOGRAPHY	**POLITICS / ECONOMICS**
PEOPLE / CULTURE	**CHANGES**

03 Your life story

1 Number these paragraphs in order for you. Add dates.

		Dates
☐	the period after school	_____
☐	pre-school days	_____
☐	other	_____
☐	late school days	_____
☐	now and the future	_____
☐	the big change	_____
☐	early school days	_____

2 Write your life story (250 words).
  a Choose a beginning (**a** or **b**).
  b Organize your story into paragraphs. Include the main events and changes in your lfe.

Beginning	My life has been ...
	    a *quite / very / completely* uneventful.
	    b *quite / very / extremely* eventful.

Paragraph 1, etc.	I was born in ...

04 Notes for a phone call

Imagine you are going on holiday to Beijing, China. Write notes for a phone call to a travel agency.

- Look at Gilly's notes and **Speak out** (*p.19*).
- Think of everything that would *really* help you to make enquiries.

05 Letter to a newspaper

Write a reply to this letter from a newspaper (150 words).

Dear Sir,

Contrary to the article by Jill Cox, not everyone welcomes technological progress. I believe we should return to a simpler way of living.

Cars, factories, computers, fast food, aeroplanes, washing machines, TVs, offices, superstores, antibiotics – all these things have made life worse for all of us.

We are no longer the same people as our parents and our grandparents. We are less healthy, less respectful and less happy than any generation before us. And it must stop – now.

Yours, Eli Weiss (Elkhart County, USA)

Paragraph 1
Say whether you agree or disagree with Eli Weiss.
Paragraph 2
Respond to the examples in the letter.
Paragraph 3
Sum up your own view.

06 Your childhood

1 Compare yourself now and as a child. Make notes under two headings:

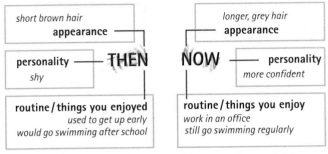

short brown hair	longer, grey hair
appearance	**appearance**
personality THEN NOW **personality**	
shy	more confident
routine / things you enjoyed	**routine / things you enjoy**
used to get up early	work in an office
would go swimming after school	still go swimming regularly

2 Write a comparison of yourself now and as a child (200 words). Say how you've changed and how you haven't changed.

07 A memorable experience

1 Complete this letter to a magazine. Use the six phrases in the box.

I thought I was going to	since then
had always been	up till then
I've never been so	now I feel as if

Dear *Soul* Magazine

My girlfriend and I were on a flight to Delhi when we were hijacked. They shot two of the passengers and forced the plane to go to Tripoli. We waited on the runway for 36 hours.
1 _____ frightened in my life. 2 _____ die.
3 _____ we 4 _____ real workaholics – desperate to earn money and pay into our pension schemes.
5 _____ , we've given up our jobs and we're about to travel round the world. We're just happy to be alive.
6 _____ I understand what life is for. And I love it!

R. Tyler, Middlestown, Yorks

2 Write a letter about a memorable experience. Use the six phrases again.

08 A message

You find this message from your flatmate on the kitchen table. Write a reply. Use the information from your diary.

Thursday, 2.30 p.m.

Hiya
What are you doing this evening? How about dinner? 7.00-ish? (you, me, Tom) – ask Laura too? Bring wine! Hope to see you later.
J

thursday

5.00 – 6.30
language class

p.m.
do shopping for weekend

09 Messages in cards

1 Match the messages with the occasions in the box.

| ill | taking exams | thanks | wedding |

A — Congratulations! Wishing you both the very best for now and always   Yours, Tim

B — Thank you very very much. I'll never forget your kindness. You're always welcome if you're ever in England. With best wishes, Vicky

C — Good luck! We'll be thinking of you! With lots of love, Pat & Simon

D — May, So sorry to hear about your leg. Hope you get well soon. Cindy

2 Write card messages for three people you know. Use phrases from *p.37* to help you.

10 Explaining directions

A friend is visiting you from abroad. Describe how to use public transport to get to your house. Explain in an informal letter, like this.

(your address)
(date)

Dear *(friend's name)*,
I'm so glad you're coming to *(town name)*. I'm sorry, I can't collect you from the airport because I'll be at work, but here's how to get to our house.

The best way is by *(train / bus / coach / taxi ...)* ...
First / next / then ..., etc.
You have to / can't *(pay on the bus)*
It takes / costs about ... / ... go every *(20 minutes)*

Looking forward to seeing you on *(date)*.
Love from *(your name)*

11 A description of an occasion

Write a vivid description of an occasion that was important to you (50 words). Use vocabulary from *p.47*.

12 'How to ...' advice

Write a short 'How to ...' article (200 words).

• Choose a topic from **Speak out** Unit 12 *(p.51)* or **Speak out** Unit 5 *(p.23)*.
• Read ... the 'How to say no' article (both parts) in the Extra activities section, Unit 12 *(pp.101/104)*.
  the advice in Unit 5 Listening 1 *(p.107)*.
• Set out your article like this:

Introduction	
Advice	(in a list)
Conclusion	

13 Describing in detail

Write a description of one of the following. Remember as many details as you can (150 words).

- the way home from school / work
- your room when you were a child
- the person you spend most time with

14 A role-model

Answer this question: 'Who makes a good role-model?' (150 words).

Introduction	Paragraph 1	Paragraph 2
What is a role-model?	Look at the results of this survey, and say what you think.	Say who you would choose, and why.

'Who demonstrates the moral values which you would like to follow?'

In a recent survey, 1,000 adults in the UK answered this question as follows:

The Guardian

own parents 88%	
doctors 78%	
teachers 78%	
sports personalities 46%	
business leaders 41%	
politicians 30%	
film / TV personalities 28%	
pop stars 20%	
none of these 2%	

15 A letter of complaint

Write a letter of complaint about a journey.

- Use Dean's notes about his plane journey on *p.61*.
- Explain what happened. Comment on technical problems, lack of information, and poor customer service. Organize your letter into paragraphs.
- Look at Megan's travel problems on *p.60* for vocabulary.
- Set out your letter like this.

(your address)
(date)

The Manager
Summer Holiday Ltd.
PO Box 104
London
W23 1RL

Dear Sir/Madam,

I am writing to complain about Flight 301 on Direct Airlines from Tel Aviv to Gatwick on 23 August this year, which I booked through your company on 15 April.

-
- etc.

As compensation for the inconvenience, I look forward to receiving a refund of the single fare from Tel Aviv to Gatwick.

Yours faithfully,

(your name)

16 An explanation

1 Read this extract from a friend's letter. Decide what you think happened.

... and he said he couldn't see me tonight because he was meeting some of his family – his parents, and a cousin – but then Teresa was walking past the restaurant and she saw him with a blonde girl, and she couldn't see his parents anywhere ... I don't know what to do.

2 Write an informal reply (100 words). Use vocabulary from *p.64*.

17 Notes for a talk

Write notes for a five-minute talk on 'Improving local leisure facilities'.

- Think of different types of leisure facilities. Note ideas for your area.

swimming pools   relaxation   parks ...
sport   sports centre ...   restaurants
entertainment   theatre ...   libraries ...   education
cinema   evening classes

- Think about who will benefit (children / teenagers / families, etc.; tourists / local people, etc.), and why.
- Set your notes out like this. Don't write sentences!

Suggestions	Reasons / Who will benefit
•	•
• etc.	• etc.

18 E-mail

Reply to this e-mail from a friend.

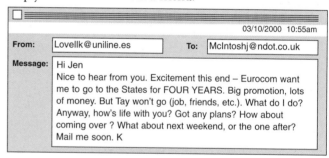

03/10/2000 10:55am

| From: | Lovellk@uniline.es | | To: | McIntoshj@ndot.co.uk |

Message:
Hi Jen
Nice to hear from you. Excitement this end – Eurocom want me to go to the States for FOUR YEARS. Big promotion, lots of money. But Tay won't go (job, friends, etc.). What do I do? Anyway, how's life with you? Got any plans? How about coming over ? What about next weekend, or the one after? Mail me soon. K

19 A newspaper report

Write a newspaper report (150 words).

- Listen to a news report on the radio / TV. Make notes.
- Look at the articles on *pp.58, 66,* and *78*.
- Write a report for an English newspaper.

20 I wish ...

Look at **Reading** *p.81*. Write a poem called 'If' (75 words).

EXTRA ACTIVITIES

02 CHANGING WORLD

Reading ex.1

Grammar ex.1

Answers to The Turning World Quiz

1c   2b   3b   4b   5b   6b   7c

03 LIFE STORY

Speaking and vocabulary ex. 2   **Student A**

1 When do these life events usually happen? Decide with Student **B**.

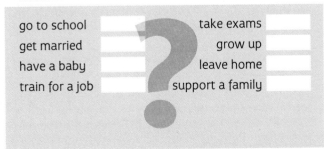

go to school		take exams	
get married		grow up	
have a baby		leave home	
train for a job		support a family	

2 In pairs, add more life events to the list.

05 A QUESTION OF LIFESTYLE

Vocabulary ex.4

1 In pairs, read and check that you understand the questions. Use a dictionary.

HEALTH TARGETS	Delivering health today
1 How important are these for good health? Number them 1–6 (1=most important). ☐ a good diet ☐ exercise ☐ freedom from stress ☐ doing things that make you happy ☐ regular health checks ☐ good sleep **2** How should you live? Tick the one you agree with most. ☐ Do everything in moderation. ☐ Do what you want and don't worry. ☐ Be strict: exercise every day, avoid sugar, don't smoke / drink, etc. ...	**3** Which are most dangerous for health? Number them 1–8 (1 = most dangerous). ☐ alcohol ☐ getting older ☐ not enough money ☐ problems at home ☐ smoking ☐ a bad diet ☐ not enough exercise ☐ stress at work / school **4** How often have you seen your doctor in the last three years? Tick one. ☐ not at all ☐ 3 – 6 times ☐ once or twice ☐ more than 6 times ☐ once a year	

2 Interview each other with the questionnaire.

Grammar ex.6   Student A

Read and remember the information.

In short, a longer life

The Chinese believe that short people live longer. They say that the taller you are, the more stress is put on your heart. Researchers explain that if you are 5% taller, then you will have 10% more skin and 16% more weight. China's oldest man, who was 131 before he died, was less than 1m 20cm.   *Top Santé*

06   CHANGE OF STATE

Reading ex.4   Student A

Read the article about Eunice. Make notes.

met John

have been married for

first lived in

have lived in England for

main problems

Marrying someone from a foreign country is seldom easy. **Annie Youngman** reports

A world apart, together

'It's difficult here. I feel I am living in the 1940s, not '90s. It's too quiet, not like Singapore.'

Eunice Jackson, 37, moved from Singapore to England 18 months ago with her husband, John. They have been married for four years.

I met my husband in Singapore at a party. We were married after a year and a half, and lived there for about two and a half years. But when my husband retired about 18 months ago, we came back to England.

It's difficult here. I feel I am living in the 1940s, not the '90s. I live in a village now, so it is entirely different from Singapore. It's too quiet. I am used to the noise. In Singapore, we lived in an apartment in a big block. Here, we have neighbours but we hardly ever see them.

The friends I have here are mainly from the tennis club. They are older than me and they all have children. Usually we only meet for tennis. They hardly ever even go out with each other. People only seem to go out with their families, if at all. After six o'clock, there aren't many people on the roads. It's very strange.

Maybe in London it might be different: I could go to the disco every night. But my husband enjoys being at home. I've hardly socialised at all.

I'm very different to my husband. For a start, I'm very noisy and he is very quiet. Sometimes he tells me to be quiet or I'll disturb the neighbours. When my sister was here, I started telling her, 'Shhh, you'll disturb the neighbours.' Perhaps I'm becoming more like the English. I hope not.

Before I left, my father said: 'Nothing is better than Singapore.'

The Guardian

08   GETTING THROUGH?

Speaking ex.2   Student A

Get Student **B** to say these words and phrases. Use any method you like, e.g. explain their meaning, mime, draw, ask questions, etc. The first pair to finish wins.

phone me   all right   have a chat   I'm not sure   I think so

10   OTHER HOUSES …

Vocabulary ex.2   Student A

1 Help Student **B**. Here are definitions of their words.
   - at precisely the right moment
   - became sad or angry
   - not allowed, forbidden
   - makes you angry; irritating
   - talked when someone else was talking
   - when people disagree and shout

2 Now turn back to *p.40* and remember all the meanings. Which pair can finish first?

11   TEMPER AND TEARS

Listening ex.3   Student A

These sentences come from Jacqui's story. Student **B** has the others. They are all mixed up. Work with Student **B** to find out what happened. Note the correct order in these boxes.

☐ ☐ ☐ ☐ ☐ ☐ ☐ ☐ ☐ ☐ ☐ ☐

a Recently I lost my temper in a clothes shop.
b 'Can't you see I'm busy?' she said.
c The assistant was going through some papers and ignoring us.
d Well, that was it! I went completely mad.
e I pointed out a pregnant woman …
f At which point, the pregnant lady turned to me and said …

Grammar ex.5

Sinead put Jenna down and moved silently down the stairs. A man was standing in the dark at the bottom. He was holding an axe, and then: 'Richard, thank God!' she cried, and threw her arms around him. And they heard a car start up, and drive away. Richard had managed to get the axe out of the man's hands, but the robber had escaped.

They turned on the lights and found that the TV and the video had gone. But they couldn't understand why the man had come into their bedroom – until they remembered Richard's Ferrari. The robber had probably come to look for the keys, which were in Richard's pocket.

12 SAYING NO

Reading ex.2 Student A

How to say 'no' nicely

An **effective** refusal should have three simple steps: acknowledge what the person wants from you, make your refusal politely but **firmly**, and then add a **sweetener**, such as "Thanks for asking me", or "I'm pleased you thought of me".

Avoid **explanations** if possible – they just give the other person something to argue against. You want to send the message that you have the right to refuse and you're choosing to do so.

Don't use **made-up** excuses too often. They send out the message that you have to have an excuse to do what you want. If someone is always taking you for granted, they'll only stop when you develop the confidence to say no.

If you find it difficult to say no, then practise in front of a mirror. Yes, it does sound silly, but it does make it easier to say it when you need to do so.

Woman's Weekly

13 BRAINPOWER

Speaking ex.1 Student A

Give your partner this memory test. Tell them to close the book and NOT look at the test.

MEMORY TEST

Read out the following tasks.

1 I'm going to tell you a short story. After the story I'd like you to repeat it to me. Then, at the end of this test, I'll ask you to say it again. This is the story:

> *A train carrying 405 passengers left London for Edinburgh. During the journey the driver became ill. However, the trainee driver with him took over the controls and completed the journey safely.*

Now, can you repeat the story?

SCORE one point each: TOTAL **6**
- [ ] train
- [ ] 405 passengers
- [ ] London to Edinburgh
- [ ] driver became ill
- [ ] trainee driver
- [ ] completed the journey

2 I'm going to say three words and I want you to repeat them straight after me. Then I'll ask you the words again in a few minutes. Here are the words:

| box | table | lamp |

Now, can you repeat the words?

SCORE one point for each word: ☐ ☐ ☐ TOTAL **3**

3 I'm going to give you a word and I would like you to spell it for me backwards. For example, SAD backwards is D-A-S. Here is the word:

| WORLD |

Can you spell it backwards?

SCORE one point for each letter in the correct place: TOTAL **5**
☐ D   ☐ L   ☐ R   ☐ O   ☐ W

4 Can you tell me the three words I gave you earlier, in question 2?

SCORE one point for each word: ☐ ☐ ☐ TOTAL **3**

5 Please subtract 7 from 100. Continue subtracting 7 until you reach 30.

SCORE one point for each correct answer: TOTAL **10**
☐ 93 ☐ 86 ☐ 79 ☐ 72 ☐ 65 ☐ 58 ☐ 51 ☐ 44 ☐ 37 ☐ 30

6 Tell me again the story in question 1.

SCORE one point each: TOTAL **6**
- [ ] train
- [ ] 405 passengers
- [ ] London to Edinburgh
- [ ] driver became ill
- [ ] trainee driver
- [ ] completed the journey

Reading the score

35	TOTAL POSSIBLE SCORE:	excellent memory
20–34	NORMAL RANGE:	good memory
15–19	BELOW AVERAGE:	some memory problems
0–14	POOR:	your memory problems probably affect your life

Please note that the test is for native English speakers: you will score less if you are doing the test in a foreign language!

Top Santé

Speak out ex.1 Pair A

Look closely at this picture for two minutes. Prepare to describe it in detail.

16 HARD TO EXPLAIN

Grammar ex.2 Student A

A homeless man, who won £25,000 on the National Lottery, has used the money to return to his birthplace in Ireland. Jim Fitzgerald of Kilburn bought his lottery ticket with his last pound coin, which was given to him by a passer-by.

The Big Issue

Speak out ex.1 Student A

Situation 1
You are Student **B**'s Mum / Dad. You told your son / daughter that they could borrow the car this evening for an important date. But now you need it because you've got an important meeting this evening. Apologize and explain the situation to them.

Situation 2
You are Student **B**'s wife. You got married six months ago. You know your husband has received at least two letters from his last girlfriend, but you haven't said anything. You feel a bit jealous and a bit suspicious because he hasn't said anything either. You are now on holiday in Tunisia with your husband. You are in a restaurant together when his ex-girlfriend walks in and sits down at another table. It can't be a coincidence!

17 WHAT WE WANT

Reading ex. 2 Student A

lifestyle: what makes you happy?

Reader's replies

1 I don't do my favourite things any more (because of work and family!). I love sleeping under the stars, seeing the sun come up, going out in the woods in thick fog or the pouring rain, playing in the snow, swimming in rivers (nude, of course), and sailing around the Mediterranean. Beauty, activity, health, and poetry! Oh, for another life!

2 There's only one thing that matters – people. Give me my family and closest friends, and I'll be happy.

3 I don't think you can be happier than you are. I think some people are born with a smile on their face and some aren't. I'm not a particularly happy person but I can get satisfaction – mostly out of my marriage and my work.

4 Dancing: music and dancing is what life's all about. I'd spend my whole life going to clubs, seeing friends, dancing, just having fun. That's what life's for, isn't it?

5 Fast cars, champagne, chocolate biscuits, long hot baths, roses, and sex.

Make notes about Replies 1 to 5 in the table.

	Things that make him/her happy	Is it a man or woman?	Is he/she happy?	Is he/she similar to you?
1				
2				
3				
4				
5				

Listening ex.6 Student A

1 You are Student **B**'s English host. You are at home, Student **B** is at school. S/he telephones you. You start: answer the phone.

2 You are in hospital. Student **B** visits you. Ask Student **B** to get you three things that you want from home. Explain how to get them, where to find them, or who Student **B** can ask. Student **B** will start.

18 FUTURE NOT GUARANTEED

Reading ex.3 Student A

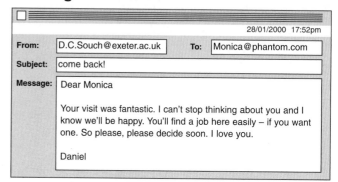

From: D.C.Souch@exeter.ac.uk
To: Monica@phantom.com
Subject: come back!
28/01/2000 17:52pm

Message:
Dear Monica

Your visit was fantastic. I can't stop thinking about you and I know we'll be happy. You'll find a job here easily – if you want one. So please, please decide soon. I love you.

Daniel

19 ALL TALK

Reading ex.4 Pair A

Read these articles. Decide what really happened.

'RAT' ROSSI

It seems that footballer Paolo Rossi, currently playing for Manchester United, has been having an affair with glamorous Russian model Cat (Ekaterina Skavronskaya).

'A REAL RAT'
'Paolo's a real rat' said Greta Shaw, friend and colleague of Bel Hansson. 'Everyone knew that Paolo was carrying on with Cat and we all thought that Bel knew about it. But obviously not.

'WILD'
'When she saw them together that night in the Groucho Club she just went wild. And who can blame her?'

Bel cancer scare

Friends of Bel Hansson yesterday came out in her defence following accusations that she was making life difficult for former boyfriend Paolo Rossi.

'She's had a hard time recently,' said Baker Tee. 'Her current record isn't selling too well and she's been in hospital two or three times over the last few months for tests for cancer.

'It's at times like these that you need the support of your friends – and you'd expect Paolo to support her too. But no. All he thinks about is himself. He couldn't take it, so he dropped her. Who needs enemies when you've got friends like that?'

HE SOUND OF BEL
HE NEW ALBUM

03 LIFE STORY

Speaking and vocabulary ex.2 Student B

1 When do these life events usually happen? Decide with Student **A**.

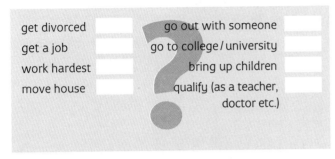

get divorced		go out with someone	
get a job		go to college / university	
work hardest		bring up children	
move house		qualify (as a teacher, doctor etc.)	

2 In pairs, add more life events to the list.

05 A QUESTION OF LIFESTYLE

Grammar ex.6 Student B

Read and remember the information.

The taller, the better

Taller people live longer, says Dr Bernard Harris at the University of Southampton. He says that a Norwegian study has found that women under 1m 45cm died younger than taller women. 'It may be genetic,' he says 'but people who have a healthy diet and lifestyle are also likely to grow taller.'

Top Santé

18 FUTURE NOT GUARANTEED

Reading ex.3 Student B

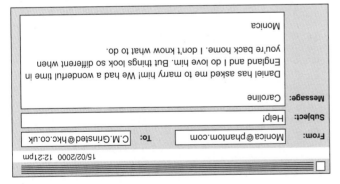

From: Monica@phantom.com To: C.M.Grinsted@hkc.co.uk
Subject: Help!
Message: Caroline

Daniel has asked me to marry him! We had a wonderful time in England and I do love him. But things look so different when you're back home. I don't know what to do.

Monica

15/02/2000 12:27pm

06 CHANGE OF STATE

Reading ex.4 Student B

Read the article about Ann. Make notes.

met David _____

were married for _____

first lived in _____

then moved to _____

main problems _____

Marrying someone from a foreign country is seldom easy. **Annie Youngman** reports

A world apart, together

'If the family came to stay, it was absolutely not allowed to ask when they were leaving.'

Ann Phiri, 57, moved to Lusaka with her Zambian husband, David. They were together for 24 years but have recently split up.

David and I met on his second day in England. He had been to school in Zambia then came to university in England. We met at Bristol and five years later we moved to Zambia. I got a job teaching in a school near Lusaka; he got a job with Anglo-American.

For a lot of women in mixed marriages, and even in Zambian marriages, the family are a problem. If the family came to stay, it was absolutely not allowed to ask when they were leaving. Sometimes they would stay for a year and the wife would have to wait on them hand and foot*. I was very lucky, though, because I had few in-laws, and David's father was lovely. The only thing I didn't

like about living in Zambia was being a long way from my family. The longest I went without going home was five years.

On the whole, Zambia was a remarkably British place. At my school they used to learn English country dancing. I never saw village life much though. That's where the real cultural differences are.

Both my sons now live in Zambia — because that is their home. Now I see them twice a year; they come over here once and I go over there once.

David says that cultural problems played a part in the breakdown of our marriage. But I am very clear in my mind that they didn't. It was never difficult for me living in Zambia. Where it went wrong was typical of any Western marriage.

The Guardian

*to wait on someone hand and foot to serve s.o. / to be like a servant or slave

08 GETTING THROUGH?

Speaking ex.2 Student B

Get Student **A** to say these words and phrases. Use any method you like, e.g. explain their meaning, mime, draw, ask questions, etc. The first pair to finish wins.

answer the phone	see you later	OK
talk to each other	I don't think so	

10 OTHER HOUSES ...

Vocabulary ex.2   Student B

1 Help Student **A**. Here are definitions of their words.
- breakfast, lunch, and dinner
- not right, not following the rules
- the biggest part of the meal
- the sweet part of the meal
- time for the main meal of the day
- cleaning the dishes and pans

2 Now turn back to *p.40* and remember all the meanings. Which pair can finish first?

11 TEMPER AND TEARS

Listening ex.3   Student B

These sentences come from Jacqui's story. Student **A** has the others. They are all mixed up. Work with Student **A** to find out what happened. Note the correct order in these boxes.

g I told her exactly what I thought of her, getting louder every second.

h After ten minutes I got fed up and asked for the assistant's help.

i 'Aren't you a bit old to be having temper tantrums?'

j who was obviously having difficulty standing for so long.

k I was in a queue at the cash desk.

l 'She'll just have to wait a bit longer.'

12 SAYING NO

Reading ex.2   Student B

How to say 'no' nicely

If you're not sure whether you want to say yes or not, then say you'll give an answer later, and refuse to discuss it further. This gives you time to decide and to prepare yourself to say no if necessary.

Use **body language** to give your words more authority: stand up straight, **straighten** your shoulders and look at the person. If you're talking on the phone, stand up – it makes you feel, and therefore sound, more confident.

If a request is **reasonable** but you don't want to do it, then offer an alternative, for example, "I don't have time on Saturday, but I could do it one night next week."

Psychologist Gael Lindenfield recommends the **'broken record'** technique, where you refuse to discuss your reasons: you simply repeat your refusal **calmly** again and again. For example: 'Thank you for the offer, but no, I'm staying at home this weekend ... I appreciate that you're disappointed but I'm staying at home this weekend ... Yes, but I've decided to stay at home this weekend.'

Woman's Weekly

13 BRAINPOWER

Speak out ex.1   Pair B

Read this story carefully for two minutes. Prepare to retell it.

Wei Ku lived in Xinjiang and worked for the Governor of the province. But he wanted a wife. Early one morning, he went for a walk and he passed the temple. On the temple steps, he saw an old man who was sitting on the steps, reading.

'Tell me what you are reading,' he said. The old man told him that he was a spirit and that his job was to arrange marriages on earth. 'Then you can tell me when I shall marry,' he said. The old man looked through his book.

'Your future wife is three years old at this moment. You will marry her when she is seventeen.' Fourteen years to wait!

'And who is she?' Wei Ku asked. The old man took him to the market and showed him an old woman. She had only one eye and she was poor and dirty. On her back was a small child. Wei Ku did not want to marry such a girl. So he arranged for a servant to kill her.

The servant went to the market with a knife to kill the child, but he could not kill her. His knife only cut her above her left eye, and he ran away.

Many years later, the Governor of Xinjiang was very pleased with Wei Ku's work and gave him his own daughter to marry. Wei Ku was very happy. His new wife was very beautiful, but her hair always covered her face above her left eye and she never moved it. When Wei Ku asked her why, she replied, 'When I was very small, a servant took me to the market one day and a madman tried to kill me.'

16 HARD TO EXPLAIN

Grammar ex.2   Student B

Strange noises have been heard from deep beneath the surface of Loch Ness, which suggests that the legendary sea monster may be more than a myth. The noises, which are similar to those of whales and dolphins, were picked up on radios by a submarine in the Loch.

The Big Issue

Speak out ex.1   Student B

Situation 1

You are Student A's child. Your Mum / Dad said you could borrow the car this evening to go to an important date. But you borrowed it this morning, while they were out, just for ten minutes, and you had a crash. It was your fault because you weren't looking carefully. The car is still at the garage. Explain the situation.

Situation 2

You are Student A's husband. You got married six months ago. You still write to your last girlfriend but you haven't seen her since your wedding. You have received three letters from her but you haven't told your wife – it was never the right time to say anything. You are now on holiday in Tunisia with your wife. You are in a restaurant together when your ex-girlfriend walks in and sits down at another table. What a coincidence!

17 WHAT WE WANT

Reading ex.2 Student B

lifestyle: what makes you happy?

Reader's replies

6 I'm happy, but I've got to achieve. And I've got to give 100 per cent or I get bored. I'm the sales director of a small and growing company and I aim to be a millionaire by the time I'm 30. I play rugby. I wanted to go professional but I had to prioritize so rugby comes after work now. I go climbing and one day I'll climb Everest. I like to look after my family and knowing they're secure feels good – and that I'm supporting them.

7 Playing the piano.

8 Being at peace with God is all that matters. With God in your heart, the world is a beautiful place. Without God, life would not be worth living.

9 I don't know what you mean. It's a luxury and I haven't got the time for it, what with looking after the kids, feeding them, earning a bit of money. I'll think about happiness when I'm old. And maybe my kids will look after me.

Make notes about Replies 6 to 9 in the table.

	Things that make him/her happy	Is it a man or woman?	Is he/she happy?	Is he/she similar to you?
6				
7				
8				
9				

Listening ex.6 Student B

1 Student A is your English host. You phone him/her from the school. Ask him/her to record something for you from the television while you are at school. Say what time, channel, and which video cassette they should use. Student A will start by answering the phone.

2 You are visiting Student B in hospital. You start: say *hello*.

18 FUTURE NOT GUARANTEED

Reading ex.3 Student C

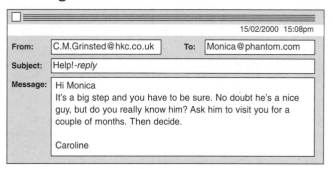

			15/02/2000 15:08pm
From:	C.M.Grinsted@hkc.co.uk	**To:**	Monica@phantom.com
Subject:	Help!-*reply*		
Message:	Hi Monica		

It's a big step and you have to be sure. No doubt he's a nice guy, but do you really know him? Ask him to visit you for a couple of months. Then decide.

Caroline

19 ALL TALK

Reading ex.4 Pair B

Read these articles. Decide what really happened.

CRAZY BEL

'Bel's crazy, everyone knows that,' said Bruce Reed, long time friend of Paolo Rossi. 'She and Paolo finished weeks ago, but she just couldn't let go'.

'She was making Paolo's life impossible. She had other lovers but always came back to Paolo. Eventually, Paolo just had to finish it.

'He and Ekaterina have been close for a long time. But Paolo was never unfaithful. I hope they can now get on with their lives. I wish them all the best.'

NICE LITTLE EARNER!
Tarsha Edwards reports

B-E-L spells trouble

The Bel and Paolo affair, it seems, just won't go away. 'I know Paolo,' said Man. United manager Colin Rushmoor. 'He wouldn't do anything to hurt anyone.'

'OTHER PROBLEMS'

This view is backed up by sources close to Paolo. 'He helped her as much as he could,' said one, 'but there were other problems, and Paolo just couldn't take it any more.'

'DRUGS'

'People have known for some time that she's been in hospital for tests,' said another. 'I assumed she was pregnant, but then I heard rumours that she was in for drugs.'

18 FUTURE NOT GUARANTEED

Reading ex.3 Student D

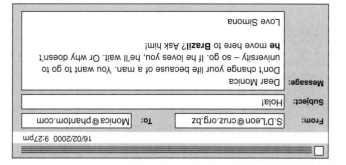

			16/02/2000 9:27pm
From:	S.D.Leon@cruz.org.bz	**To:**	Monica@phantom.com
Subject:	Hola!		
Message:	Dear Monica		

Don't change your life because of a man. You want to go to university – so go. If he loves you, he'll wait. Or why doesn't **he** move here to **Brazil**? Ask him!

Love Simona

TAPESCRIPT

01 ALL IN THE MIND

1 A Excuse me, sorry. Can you tell me where the International Department is, please?
  B Yes, sure, it's on the first floor of C Block.

2 C Hello, hi
  D Hiya, all right?
  C How're things?

3 E Hear you been to Spain.
  F Yeah, yeah, it was great.
  E Good. How long for?
  F Just for a week.
  E Not long enough then, eh!
  F No!

4 G Hi.
  H Hi there.
  G Kevin ...?
  H Barber.
  G Hello, hi. Come in. Pleased to meet you.
  H This is Brian.
  I Hello there.
  G Hello Brian. My name's Will. Please come in. Er, first of all, would you like a cup of tea or coffee?
  H Love one. Thought you'd never ask.
  I No, it's alright.

5 J Hi ...
  K Hi. Oh hi! Haven't seen you for ages. What've you been up to?
  J Oh not much, been quite busy you know ... And you?
  K Yeah, me too, anyway, nice to see you, ...

02 CHANGING WORLD

Changes in Afghanistan

Presenter Afghanistan's Taliban movement took power in Kabul in 1996. It has already banned television, music, and cinemas, because, it says, they are un-Islamic. James Foreman reports.

Reporter This is just one of the many attempts by the Taliban to free Afghanistan from the influence of film and music. In the past, they have smashed and even publicly hanged television sets, and they have burnt cinema films. But up till now they've allowed people to keep TV sets and video machines as long as they weren't using them. These changes do not have public support. Large numbers of people, particularly the young, are still watching videos and satellite channels. Shop owners and private citizens have been ordered to throw out their TVs, videos, and satellite receivers within fifteen days.

Talking about Hong Kong

Um, the population of Hong Kong is, um, it's about six million. Um and there are a large number of islands, the New Territories and Kowloon are actually part of the mainland of China but Hong Kong Island is actually separate from that, um, the population, there tend to be well, open spaces and then very densely populated areas. As far as the climate's concerned, in the summer, um, it reaches 34 degrees but the humidity can be sometimes up to about 100 per cent so it, it's very very sticky ...

Um, as far as the food is concerned, it's a wonderful place, I mean, I think there are something like 19 thousand restaurants for a population of six million, which is incredible – it's the most incredible place ...

Um it's the sort of place where everybody has to be responsible for themselves financially, there's no social security network so people try to make their fortunes and there is an emphasis on money ...

... but most people are really friendly. I think anyway. Umm. Then, as far as the food's concerned, it's very, very mixed, it's the kind of place where you can find Japanese, Chinese, Thai, French, and Italian restaurants all in the same street - and everyone's eating in the Burger King round the corner!

03 LIFE STORY

An interview with Miguel

Interviewer What was your life like when you were growing up there?

Miguel Well, when I was growing up in the jungle from six, seven years old, my dad trained me, took me fishing, hunting, canoeing and that kind of thing, so basically, I was trained to survive in the jungle.

Interviewer So how did you get to your first school, then, to get your education?

Miguel Well, I didn't speak Spanish at the time, so I travelled for four or five days in a canoe from my village to the closest city, which is called Pucallpa.

Interviewer And there you were taken in by a Peruvian family, there, weren't you?

Miguel Yes, that's right, yes, they gave me a place to stay and food in exchange for work, so I worked during the day and went to school at night.

Interviewer And you taught yourself Spanish and you then went on to further education in Lima.

Miguel That's right.

Interviewer How did you live when you were in Lima?

Miguel When I was in Lima I was seventeen years old and I couldn't find work 'cause I didn't have any skills and also because I was an Indian. That didn't help at all. So, I was on the street for two months, you know, eating leftover food from the Chinese restaurant you know, around three in the morning, they used to throw the food away, you know, so that's how I survived for a couple of months, but later on I found some missionaries and I think they felt sorry for me and they offered me a place to stay and a job, so from '87 to 1989 I studied theology and linguistics for three years, and I finished in 1990 - and that's how my life started.

Interviewer And you then got a scholarship to study in Texas, didn't you, and then a scholarship to study in Oxford ...

Miguel Right.

04 SOMETHING TO DO

Magnus says what he enjoys

We've just bought a car and it's just so easy to jump in the car and go to wherever we want to go, you don't have to wait on buses or trains or, um, I do enjoy other things as well, er, I enjoy swimming whenever I get a chance to, in the swimming pool, and jumping off the diving board, I think it's a great way to relax, er I really enjoy swimming, it's just great to be in the water and just, just let yourself go free, it's a world of your own.

The reason why I enjoy music so much, er, especially dance music, is because I've got this, er, great sense of rhythm – and I love drumming, so it's great when I get a chance to get behind a drum kit and, you know.

My friend Ted owns a music shop, er, selling all sorts of, er, musical instruments, so if ever I do have the time, I occasionally like to go down to, to Ted's shop and he's always got a drum kit there and a few guitars so we, we quite enjoy a session now and again, whenever I get the time.

Phoning the tourist office

Clerk Visitor information, can I help you?

Gilly Oh, yes, hello, I wonder if you can. Um, I'm thinking of coming over to Boston in August and I was wondering if you could give me some, um, general information about sightseeing, etc.

Clerk OK

Gilly I was wondering if you could tell me, late August, er what's the weather like at that time?

Clerk Oh it's almost impossible to tell but, you know, it could be humid, and hot – into the nineties and above.

Gilly Oh fine, OK, so, um, with regard to swimming, er, do you have many beaches or ...?

Clerk Oh, I wouldn't go into the city to swim.

Gilly Oh right.

Clerk You can walk on the beaches here, but er, to swim, I would go north or south of Boston about an hour or so.

Gilly I see, OK, that's fine. OK. Regarding hotels, should I book in advance or can we just sort of arrive and book once we arrive?

Clerk	In Boston?
Gilly	Yeah, in Boston itself, yes.
Clerk	Oh, no, you want to make a reservation for August probably now,
Gilly	**Right**, er. OK. Could you also recommend, um, the main things there are to see?
Clerk	Now, that's, like, Boston's a major metropolitan city, I mean, er, we're known for our history, with the American Revolution, er, we have many museums,
Gilly	Uh huh
Clerk	There's the Children's Museum, the Science Museum, The Museum of Fine Arts, the New England Aquarium,
Gilly	**Excellent** ...
Clerk	... excellent shopping, clothes stores, book stores, then parks, and just half an hour outside Boston there are the forests and lakes of New England.
Gilly	**I see**, so, so it would sort of, suit most people with different interests
Clerk	I would think so.
Gilly	**Good**, right well that's lovely
Clerk	We're not little you know, not a little town,
Gilly	OK, well, thank you very much.
Clerk	You're very welcome.

05 A QUESTION OF LIFESTYLE

 1

What time should people go to bed?

* Early to bed, early to rise.
* An early night is better for you.
* It's better to sleep before midnight.

What's the best amount of sleep to have?

* Just sleep when you want to sleep, so if you want to sleep in the afternoon, then sleep. Like a cat. Just like a cat. I would like to have about eleven hours.
* Nine or ten hours would be nice.
* I like eight hours. My husband says I don't need eight hours but I reckon I do.
* They say for old people, it's about four hours.
* The best amount of sleep to have is the least. I think you function better on six hours rather than ten.
* The more you sleep, the more tired you get, I reckon.

What causes insomnia, do you think?

* I can't go to sleep if I'm too tired. I feel as though I'm absolutely exhausted and I just can't sleep.

What should you do if you can't sleep?

* Hot milk.
* I get up and have a hot cup of tea. It's full of caffeine surely isn't it, tea? I'm from Sri Lanka so we have the best tea only in Sri Lanka.
* Whisky. How much? A couple of doubles. That'll soon put you to sleep.

2 Having a health check

Nurse	Are you a smoker?
Will	Not really, no, um, I, I do occasionally smoke a cigar and it probably comes to about one a month.
Nurse	Are you tempted to smoke more sometimes?
Will	Um, occasionally, I suppose.
Nurse	I mean, if you keep it to one a month, that's probably OK, but ...
Nurse	Do you drink any alcohol on a regular basis?
Will	Er, yes, I do, um. You want to know how much.
Nurse	Every, every day?
Will	It varies an awful lot. Um. At the moment I'm probably having a drink every day.
Nurse	Just one?
Will	A couple of glasses of wine.
Nurse	Well that's fine. Two glasses of wine every day is fine for a man. That's fourteen units a week.
Will	Oh, that's good.

06 CHANGE OF STATE

4 Friday nights

W1	We're not interested in the men.
W2	The music is what's important. All these people come here together to listen to the music. And you've got something in common.
W3	Well, it's just a good night out, isn't it? It's exciting. The best part of the week.
W4	The big attraction, really, was the opposite sex. You'd go out to find a partner for the weekend. So, you'd go out about five o'clock and walk along chatting with your friends, but really you were looking at the boys. And then round about five-thirty sixish, the road would fill up with people. All the pub doors would be open, but we weren't allowed in, and you'd pick up a boy to go to the cinema with or maybe to a dance. And then you'd walk home afterwards and you'd normally get home by midnight.
M1	The evening starts about eight nine o'clock, we usually meet up in a pub then go straight to a club where we usually just spend most of the time on the dance floor just dancing.
M2	The important thing is to wear something that's really comfortable, that's not going to get too hot ... The whole point of going out on a Friday night is to enjoy lots of different experiences so you don't just go to one place, you go to a couple of clubs, and maybe a few different bars.
W5	You'd go out in the morning, to the shops, buy the material for a dress, then you'd make it in the afternoon and you would probably wear it in the evening. I used to mainly wear circular skirts and very high heels.
M1	The atmosphere is great, the street is alive with colours, the colours of the clothes is quite incredible. The bars are full, there's music blasting onto the streets, there's people outside, there's laughter, there's arguments. It's just an incredible experience, really.

07 TAKING CHANCES

1 Conversation 1

A	We're so safe these days and life is so easy
B	Yeah, that's true, it is easy
A	And I don't think it's good for us
B	No, nor do I,
A	'cause danger and risk are, natural,
B	- normal
A	- aren't they? But we need the chance to, to face our fear to develop confidence
B	Yeah, I agree,
A	I remember I used to be terrified of water, and then I got, or a friend of mine found this company called Real Dreams who arrange holidays, experiences to help people to achieve their dream, whatever it is, their you know lifetime dream,
B	Oh, that's,
A	and mine was, that I'd always wanted to swim with dolphins, but I was terrified of water so you know there was no chance
B	No.
A	But Real Dreams arranged this trip for me to Miami, to a place called, er, Dolphin Plus in Miami, to this dolphin reserve, and there they were. Two dolphins. This beautiful blue sea
B	Oh, lovely
A	and of course I was nervous but I was just so excited I just walked into the sea and these dolphins came up to me and they, they helped me,
B	Really?
A	Yeah, they, they helped me to swim, they supported me in the water, and they played. And I just spent hours and hours just playing with these dolphins, and all my fears went. I was swimming and I wasn't frightened any more. I felt so relaxed, and, and the fear just went away and now I feel like a completely different person. It was wonderful.
B	That's great.

Conversation 2

A	Everything was really peaceful at first
B	Yeah?
A	We were going down this river and there were hills and woods on both sides, and then I heard the sound of water rushing and it got louder and louder and we got faster and faster and then for a split second I was suddenly terrified.
B	I can imagine
A	But there was no time to think. There was water everywhere and and we were going really really fast and you just had to concentrate on getting that boat to go the right way between the rocks. It was the most exciting, involving experience I've ever had.
B	Wow.
A	You just can't get that sort of experience in everyday life.
B	No. No, that's right.
A	And then we entered a quiet pool, and it all just stopped and I, I felt completely ... you know, totally satisfied. I'd been completely involved the whole time.
B	Yeah.
A	I think everyone needs to have that sort of experience.
B	Yes, so do I. 'Cause I get the same sort of thing from skiing.
A	Really?
B	Yes, 'cause when you're going really fast ...

Conversation 3

A	I don't like the cold, I don't like the wet and I don't much like walking really.
B	No, nor do I. Especially up mountains in bad weather
A	And carrying enormous packs on your back. I hate it.
B	Yeah, me too.
A	We had to do all of that stuff at my school.
B	Did you?
A	I can remember one particularly awful time. We went to, oh some mountains somewhere, and they left us there with a map and a tent and enough food for an afternoon.
B	Oh God.
A	And said see you in two days, and, oh it was a nightmare.
B	And did you?
A	What, meet them in two days? No, we got lost, and we were completely exhausted, wet, cold and miserable
B	Oh dear.
A	And I felt, I felt relieved when they found us 'cause we were frightened by then – and hungry.
B	Well yeah,
A	But they were so, you know they thought it was funny, and I just felt embarrassed and humiliated.
B	God, that sounds awful.

08 GETTING THROUGH?

🔊1 Call 1 Tom calls Gareth

Gareth	Hello
Tom	Hi, Gareth. It's Tom.
Gareth	Hello Tom.
Tom	How are you doing?
Gareth	Oh not so bad. And you?
Tom	Yeah, not too bad ... Listen, are you watching the game tonight?
Gareth	Sorry?
Tom	Are you going to watch the football tonight?
Gareth	Um, yeah, I think so.
Tom	At home?
Gareth	No, I'll probably go and watch it in the pub, with Mike probably.
Tom	Oh, great. So do you know where you're gonna go?
Gareth	I'm not sure. Um. Mike's ringing me later. But we'll probably go into town.
Tom	Right.
Gareth	Yeah. Mike's finishing work at five and then he's gonna give me a call. So I'll call you back later, shall I?
Tom	Sorry?
Gareth	I'll call you back later, shall I?
Tom	Well, I'm not at home – I'm just about to go home now.
Gareth	Right, well, I'll give you a call there then, probably around six.
Tom	OK.
Gareth	All right then.
Tom	Fine.
Gareth	Is Laura coming out?
Tom	Um, I expect so, yes.
Gareth	So things are going well with you and her then, are they?
Tom	Um, I guess so.
Gareth	Good. Er, anyway, I'll give you a call later, yeah?
Tom	Excellent.
Gareth	All right then, see you later.
Tom	See you. Bye.
Gareth	Bye.

Call 2 Tom calls Nick

Mother	Double five three six four oh.
Tom	Hi, can I speak to Nick, please?
Mother	Yes, who's calling?
Tom	It's Tom.
Mother	Oh, hello Tom, how are you?
Tom	I'm very well thank you, how are you?
Mother	Fine thanks. Enjoying yourself?
Tom	Having a great time, yup, ... thanks.
Mother	Excellent. OK I'll just call him. Hold on.
Tom	Thank you very much.
Nick	Hello
Tom	Hi Nick.
Nick	How're you doing mate?
Tom	Not too bad.
Nick	Cool.
Tom	Um, I can come tonight
Nick	Really? Oh, fantastic.
Tom	Yeah
Nick	Um, right, um, how, how're you gonna get there?
Tom	Um, well, my mum can probably drive me over to your house
Nick	Well, everybody's cycling up.
Tom	Oh are they?
Nick	So we can meet you there.
Tom	OK, whereabouts?
Nick	You know the carpark, the carpark on the top as you go over the hill?
Tom	Yeah.
Nick	We're meeting there about, um, half eight

Tom	All right then, well I'll meet you there then.
Nick	Great.
Tom	Excellent, OK. So about half past eight in the carpark.
Nick	Yeah.
Tom	Excellent.
Nick	And if we're a bit late, don't worry, 'cause we're slow ...
Tom	Oh, right, OK. All right.
Nick	And bring something to drink, some beer, wine and stuff.
Tom	Yeah. I will do. And, er, is it OK if Laura comes?
Nick	Oh, yeah, course.
Tom	All right then.
Nick	OK.
Tom	OK. See you later.
Nick	See you.
Tom	Bye.
Nick	Bye.

09 INCIDENTS AND ACCIDENTS

🔊1

1

Clare	... Let's have a look
Paul	Fantastic socks
Jem	Wow, they're wicked man
Rosa	They're birthday socks.
Paul	They're cool.
Clare	I didn't know it was your birthday.
Jem	When was it?
Rosa	Yesterday.
Clare	Really? Well Happy Birthday
Paul	Yeah. Happy Birthday Rosa
Jem	So what did you do? Have you been out on the town yet?
Rosa	No, no, nothing, yet. We're going out tomorrow night.
Clare	Where are you going?
Rosa	Donatello's, then on to a club.
Clare	Oh well, have a really good time.
Rosa	Thanks, yeah, we will.

2

Helen	Hello Peter ...
Peter	Hi.
Helen	... what's happened? Is it broken?
Peter	... yeah, well, ...
Helen	Oh dear. How did it happen?
Peter	... ya, well, it was really stupid. Like, I was coming down the stairs, with a box yeah?
Helen	What at home?
Peter	Yeah, with this box right, like this, so I couldn't see where I was going. But ...
Helen	Oh no ...
Peter	.. Jenny'd left one of her balls
Helen	... one of her toys
Peter	and I just fell
Helen	Oh how awful. I am sorry. Is it, I mean, how bad is it?
Peter	Broken in three places.
Helen	Oh God. That's terrible ...
Peter	Yes
Helen	... Well I hope you get better soon.

3

Sarah	No, that's all right. Oh, hello Stuart.
Stuart	Hello Sarah
Sarah	How are you getting on?
Stuart	All right.
Sarah	I hear your exams didn't go too well.
Stuart	No. I failed two of them.
Sarah	Oh, bad luck. What a shame. I am sorry. What does it mean, though, I mean, what do you do next?
Stuart	Well, decide if I want to re-take them.
Sarah	And do you?

4

Andy	... going quite well really, I mean. It's a bit boring at times, you know. But you get that with any job.
Nick	Yeah. Like mine. I've just applied for another job
Andy	Really? Is it I mean, what sort of
Nick	Well it's quite good really, it's for manager of the computer services department of a building, you know, construction company. It's quite a big one down here, called Bride's.
Andy	Oh, yeah?
Nick	And I've got an interview.
Andy	Really?
Nick	On Wednesday.
Andy	Well, brilliant. Congratulations, well done.
Nick	Well, have to see – wait if I get the job first.
Andy	Yeah, well these days, it's difficult enough getting an interview, I mean that's pretty good going.
Nick	Yeah, well, we'll see.
Andy	Yeah. Good luck! I hope it goes well.
Nick	Thanks. So do I.

5

Matt	Hello Helen.
Helen	Matt, hi.
Matt	Haven't seen you for ages. What've you been up to?
Helen	I've been to Toronto.
Matt	Toronto? What took you there?
Helen	I got married – married a Canadian!
Matt	You didn't! Well, congratulations, that's great. How about a drink?
Helen	All right ...

6

Dan	This is really delicious. Mm. I just love these mushrooms. I've never really had them like this before.
Joanna	Well, thank you. And this wine is lovely.
Dan	Good. I'm glad you like it. Listen, I just want to say thank you.
Joanna	Oh, there's no ...
Dan	No. I really mean it. Thank you very much indeed for having me. You've been really kind and I've really enjoyed my stay here.
Joanna	Well, you're very welcome. It's been lovely having you.
Dan	And if you ever, you know, if you and Sam ever come to the States, you will let me know, won't you?
Joanna	Oh, it seems
Dan	You'd like it out there.

10 OTHER HOUSES, OTHER RULES

🔊1 Rules for eight

Alice	They do tend to be a bit slow, especially at dinnertime and so the rule is, at mealtimes, if you're not here when we're ready to start, then you don't get pudding. Because this does tend to get them down for dinner on time – which is you know, important when there's eight people.
Child (8)	Um, the rules at the table are that you you mustn't interrupt when somebody's talking – you've got to wait till they've finished otherwise it causes arguments, and it, it just, it's quite annoying when someone keeps interrupting you.
Child (13)	Yeah, and after dinner, we've got to help with the washing-up, 'cause with eight of us, there's a lot to do, but sometimes, it's a bit annoying, if you've got things to do and stuff, but ... it's all right I suppose. Most of the time.

Alice	Our biggest arguments are about television, because television is banned in the week and they're only allowed to watch it at weekends, 'cause, um, they, they're very lucky to live in the countryside, and if you send them outside, it only takes them five minutes to find something to do, something that makes them feel much better than watching TV.
Child (13)	But you don't let us watch the news, even at weekends
Alice	No, because I think there're a lot of very horrific images …
Child (13)	But I'm thirteen and I'm not allowed to watch the news. I want to know what's going on in the world.
Alice	I've never stopped you seeing newspapers or listening to the radio but I do stop you seeing horrific images …
Alice	The trouble is, they're reaching an age where nobody else ever has to do the washing-up, everybody else is allowed to stay up till midnight, everybody else is allowed to watch TV, and you just have to say, 'Well, that's very interesting, but 'other houses, other rules'.

11 TEMPER AND TEARS

🔊1 Conversation 1

A Um, excuse me.
B Yes?
A I'm afraid this coffee's cold.
B Oh, I'm sorry.
A I'd like another one, please.
B Yes, of course.
A Thank you.

Conversation 2

C Um, I bought this er, yesterday, and I'm afraid it's too small. I'd like to change it, please.
D Have you got your receipt?
C I'm afraid not, no, but I've got the bag and everything.
D Well, I'm sorry but we don't change things without a receipt.
C Well, I understand that, but I want to change it, even though I haven't got the receipt.
D I'll have to see the manager.
C That's fine.
E Er, good morning. I understand you'd like to change this pullover.
C Yes, that's right.
E Have we got the right size in stock, do you know?
C Yes, you have.
E Well, I don't see any problem with that. … I'm sorry about the …

🔊3 One of those days

I don't lose my temper very often but when I do, I really explode.

Just a couple of months ago, I had 'one of those days'. I'd cleaned the fridge the night before and woke up to find a huge puddle of water on the floor. So I cleared it up and was late for work – which made me late for a lunch date.

The friend I was meeting irritated me because she'd forgotten to bring back a dress she'd borrowed, which I'd planned to wear to a party that night.

So I went home at six o'clock to find something else to wear. But when I got back to my flat I couldn't find my door keys!

After looking through my bag several times, I tipped everything out on to the pavement and my keys fell

straight down a drain! I went mad then, shouting and screaming at the top of my voice.

I didn't go to the party that night. By the time I got to bed, I was exhausted.

🔊4

Recently I lost my temper in a clothes shop. I was in a queue at the cash desk, and the assistant was going through some papers and ignoring us.

After ten minutes I got fed up and asked for the assistant's help. I pointed out a pregnant woman who was obviously having difficulty standing for so long.

'Can't you see I'm busy?' she said, 'She'll just have to wait a bit longer'. Well, that was it! I went completely mad and told her exactly what I thought of her, getting louder every second.

At which point the pregnant lady turned to me and said, 'Aren't you a bit old to be having temper tantrums?'

12 SAYING NO

🔊1

1 M Hi Mike.
S Oh hi Sebastian.
M Busy, isn't it?
S Hell.
M Do you fancy a drink?
S Sorry. I'd love to but I've got to get home.
M Stuff to do.
S Stuff to do, yeah.
M Shame
S Yeah well, see you tomorrow, anyway
M Yeah, see you.

2 M I think I'm going to get out now.
F Yeah. Me too.
M Would you like to go for a coffee afterwards?
F That would be nice. But not in here.
M No?
F Coffee's dreadful. There's an Italian bar not far though. We could go there.
M Oh yes. Oh yes. That's a good idea.
F Right. I'll see you in the foyer then. About ten minutes? Got to dry my hair.
M OK. In the hall. Where we came in.

3 M It was the same in Mongolia.
S Yes. Quite an experience.
M Mmm. Um, look, Simona. I was wondering. Er, would you like to come round for dinner? You know. You could meet Hilary.
S Oh. Really? That's very nice of you. I'd love to. Thank you.
M OK, how about, um, Friday night? Or Saturday?
S Which is preferable for you?
M Well, it's, I don't know really. It doesn't really matter. Well let's say Friday.
S That would be great.
M OK. Round about half past seven?

4 C Oh, hi, Joanna!
J Yes? Oh Clare, hi.
C Hi, look, um, Diana and me, we're going to the seaside tomorrow. Would you like to come?
J Oh, that's kind of you. I'm afraid I can't, I'm sorry. I've got something on tomorrow.
C Oh, well never mind.
J It's a shame. Maybe another weekend?
C Well, yes, why not? Perhaps we could arrange something.
J Yes that would be nice.
C OK, well um, I'll see you later then.
J Yes see you. Bye.

5 F Listen, John, I was wondering, we're having a barbecue on Saturday, just having you know a few friends over. I was wondering if you'd like to come.
J Oh that would be very nice. Thank you.
F Oh good. Well we're starting about six thirty, seven, so, any time after that really.
J Well, smashing, thank you very much, I'll really, … um …
F Was there someone you'd like to er
J Well, if I
F Certainly, very welcome, what's the er?
J Rachel.
F Oh, right, well by all means, sure.
J Oh, right, then I'll um, thank you very much.
F We'll see you on Saturday then.
J Yes.

13 BRAINPOWER

🔊1 Talking about memory

Mick What's the article about?
Lynn It's basically about memory and it says that you've got three memories: short term, medium term, long term.
Mick Mm
Lynn Um, they say that short term memory lasts only a few seconds, thirty seconds I think they said, so you just sort of read something, I suppose and you, you remember the beginning of the sentence just until you get to the end of the sentence,
Mick Mmm
Lynn And then um, medium term memory, the example they give is something like trying to remember that you've got to buy bread
Mick Like a sort of a shopping list of things to do
Lynn So some time later you buy bread, and then when you've done it you don't need to restore, er to store that memory any longer and so it's erased.
Mick Just, sort of a day-to-day management,
Lynn Yes, but they don't say how long, how long it lasts but I suppose you remember it as long as you need it, and then you forget it.
Mick Mm.
Lynn Er, then long term memory, um, they're talking about major events that happen in your life such as your wedding, um, that you remember, and er, then things that are there all the time, like, er, the faces of your your friends and family and things that are constantly around you
Mick And you never forget them.
Lynn Yes, I suppose so, permanent memory.

🔊2

Mick And you never forget them.
Lynn Yes, I suppose so, permanent memory.
Mick Are there any …, are …, are any memories really permanent?
Lynn Well, they talk about what happens when you get older. You don't actually forget things, you just find it harder to learn new things, and you start to get confused.
Mick Sorry?
Lynn You get confused.
Mick Ah, so, it's … brain cells dying and so on.
Lynn Well, not exactly, they they say that cells do die as you get older, but that's not the problem, because you've still got more cells than you need to remember,
Mick Mm, mm, mm
Lynn Um but the problem is the the, I can't quite remember the right word, the

	communication between the cells? the connections between the cells?
Mick	Interconnections?
Lynn	Yeah, I can't remember the right word, but that's the problem, it's not the fact that the cells are dying, um, because you've got enough cells to to remember, it's that they stop communicating.
Mick	Mm
Lynn	It's the connections between the cells that's the problem.

14 GIVING IMPRESSIONS

⊙1 Discussing Einstein

Interviewer	So how did Einstein first get interested in science?
Dr James	Well, in those days, there was a tradition that Jewish families would take in a poor Jewish student for a meal once a week, and they had a student who was studying science and he would talk to Albert about science and what was going on.
Interviewer	And it went on from there. But there's this idea that Einstein was a lazy, rather slow child. Is that true?
Dr James	Yes and no. I mean, he was lazy at things he wasn't interested in, and he hated the school system in Germany in that time, where children were punished for giving the wrong answer and things like that, but he was interested in things that interested him. There's a famous story about him being given a compass when he was a small boy, and how he was fascinated by the way the compass always pointed north – he was deeply interested in all that stuff, but then he had to go to school and learn things by rote and he just lost interest. He just hated the system and this applied when he went to university in Zurich, I mean he just didn't go to any lectures. He spent all the time in the library reading about things that he was interested in and when the exams came along, he had to borrow a friend's notes and he only just passed the exams as a result.
Interviewer	With his poor exam results, it's not surprising that Einstein found it hard to get a job, but some friends helped him find work at the Swiss patent office in Bern. In the mornings, Einstein worked on patents, but in the afternoons, he began working on the theories that would revolutionize science. And his greatest contributions to science, the special theory of relativity, and the general theory of relativity, came from ideas he had while sitting at his desk in the patent office.

⊙2

Interviewer	But last year some of Einstein's letters were sold in New York and they tell a different story about Einstein. Einstein met a Hungarian woman called Mileve Marij at the University of Zurich, where they were students. But Mileve did not complete her studies. She became pregnant with Einstein's child while they were still at university and before they were married. She returned to Hungary to give birth to a daughter, Lisel. Einstein never saw the child: she simply disappeared from their lives.

Einstein married Mileve in 1903 and they had two sons. In 1914, the family moved from Zurich to Berlin and Einstein was made professor at the University. It was there that he began an affair with his cousin, Elsa. They lived together for a year, and then Einstein divorced Mileve in 1918. He won the Nobel Prize for Physics in 1921. Einstein died in 1955.

15 JOURNEYS

⊙1 Problems on the plane

Presenter	Well, eventually, Dean, you took off seventeen hours late, which is quite a delay, isn't it?
Dean	That's right, seventeen hours late, and then about two hours into the flight, we were told we'd have to divert to Athens due to a problem with the engines.
Presenter	So you touched down in Athens. What happened then?
Dean	We were then told that we weren't allowed to leave the plane, and we were finally taken off the plane probably about thirty forty minutes later, into the Athens terminal, where we were given really no information at all for about forty minutes.
Presenter	Now is it right that at one point the passengers actually refused to get back on the flight because there'd been so many problems with it?
Dean	Yeah, the, the majority of passengers were refusing to get on the plane because you don't really want to get back in the same aircraft when you were delayed in the first place due to a technical fault and had to land due to a technical fault.
Presenter	So what's the latest now, Dean?
Dean	We're at the airport now, people are checking onto a flight from an airline called Peach airlines. That's supposedly taking off at about three o'clock Athens time, and should be flying straight to Gatwick, so, I mean, by the time we land in England, if we land on time, this flight will have been delayed forty hours.
Presenter	What do you think of the service, then, so far?
Dean	I think it's appalling, is the only word I can think to describe it, severe, severe lack of information I don't think any one of the passengers has seen anyone or spoken to anyone from the airline, and I think the most disgusting event is to see the crew of the plane being taken off to hotels before any of the passengers ...
Presenter	It's ridiculous isn't it?
Dean	I think it's their duty to make sure all the passengers, especially when there's a lot of children on this flight, a lot of young children, a lot of families you know, and the crew are just going off. I do think that's wrong.

16 HARD TO EXPLAIN

⊙2

In the Guilin Mountains of China, residents simply yell for rain when they need it. At the foot of the mountains are a group of pools called The Mysterious Lakes, where the air is hot and wet, and whenever anyone stands by them and speaks in a loud voice, rain immediately follows. The louder the yell, the heavier the rain; the longer the yell, the longer it lasts.

⊙3 Something strange

Clare	... and she was having dinner when she suddenly felt really sick and she knew something was wrong, and at that very moment, her husband, who was thousands of miles away, had that awful accident. Which I think is amazing. I mean it's not, it's not just coincidence.
Andy	Hmm. Well I mean, it is very unusual but ... you see I just don't think that there's anything strange going on. I mean, it is strange. But it doesn't mean that there are strange forces at work, does it? I mean, how do they know it was 'at the very same moment' – it could be pure chance and ...
Clare	But why? Why can't it be something else? I mean, I'm not saying I understand it, but it may be that there's some, I don't know, some force that connects people, ...
Andy	But, yes, maybe, but I'm just saying that it's not very likely, is it?
Clare	Hmm ...
Andy	Look, I'm sorry. It's just that I can't believe that we have strange powers, I mean, if we do have these powers, then surely we'd know about them - we'd use them all the time.
Clare	I'm not saying that we can just use it, this power, any time we want to, but it could be that, I don't know, that some people can use it and some people can't.
Andy	I just don't see why we need to invent mysterious powers and so on, when strange things happen by chance sometimes anyway. It just doesn't make any sense to me.

17 WHAT WE WANT

⊙2 Part 1

Mick	Damn. I forgot to set the video to record.
Lynn	Oh. Oh, Andy? Can I borrow the phone? Can I phone home? I want to ask ...
Andy	Yes, of course.
Lynn	... somebody to video a couple of things.
Andy	Sure, go ahead.
Lynn	Oh, and have you got, can I borrow a TV mag? Or today's paper or something?
Andy	Here's the paper.
Lynn	That's great. Thanks. Hi, is that Sean? Um, Sean, could you do me a favour, could you video a couple of things for me?

Part 2

Lynn	Hi, is that Sean? Um, Sean, could you do me a favour, could you video a couple of things for me?
Mick	Three things
Lynn	Three things. ... Yeah. ... OK. Um. One, could you video the Final, this afternoon. I think it's um, it's on Sky Sports 1 from three till six thirty. Actually, you could just put the VideoPlus number in, it's, er, seven nine two, seven seven two seven. Um, could you not use the, the tape that's in there – I want to watch that. Um, but, if you could just find a blank tape and use that? ... Yeah. There should be some new ones on top of the video. ... OK, and then, um, could you also record Star Trek, that's, er two six five, seven four six on BBC 2. ... Yeah, it can go on the same tape. And then, um, on Channel Four, if you could record Hostage? That's at 9.00, um, number one two nine, two oh. ... Yes, that's it. ... Great. Thanks. Bye. ... Ya, he's fine, he's, he'll record all those. Honestly.

18 FUTURE NOT GUARANTEED

🔲1 **A news story**

Presenter If you look out into the night sky, imagine a giant asteroid, a mile in diameter, orbiting the Earth. It is out there and according to scientists, it could have a very nasty landing on Earth in thirty years' time. Known as asteroid XF11, it is certain to pass close to the Earth but there's only a one in a thousand chance that it will hit us, releasing energy equal to thousands of atomic bombs. If you really want to be scared, you can book a seat to see Hollywood blockbuster Deep Impact. In a moment I'll be speaking to the director, but first, the story.

Reporter Stephen Spielberg's uncannily caught the public mood again. His film, Deep Impact, tells of a world about to be hit by giant asteroids. It's being released just as scientists say a giant asteroid called XF11 might hit us in two thousand and twenty-eight. At worst, scientists say, it could kill a billion people and wipe out civilization. There's no doubt the Earth is in the danger zone, though the asteroid could just miss, but if you're alive in two thousand and twenty-eight, statisticians reckon you're more likely to be hit by the asteroid than killed in a car accident.

🔲3

Daniel ... just can't concentrate somehow. Long day today anyway.

Steve Are you coming out this evening?

Daniel Er. I'm not sure if I can. Where are you going?

Steve Don't know. The pub I expect.

Daniel Oh, I don't think so. Got my first language class this evening. Not sure what time we finish.

Steve What's that?

Daniel Portuguese. For beginners.

Steve It's really difficult, isn't it, Portuguese?

Daniel Don't think so. Hope not: I've only got eight weeks to learn it in. Then I'm off to Brazil.

Steve How long for?

Daniel Well, forever. Hopefully.

Steve Really? What, with, er, what's her name?

Daniel Monica. Yeah, that's right.

Steve Well, good luck. What, what are you going to do out there?

Daniel Oh, I'm sure I'll find a computer company over there, or, ... at least I hope so. And anyway Monica will help. But who cares? I'm in love.

Steve I don't know if you're lucky or just stupid.

Daniel Both, I should think, I mean. I mean I know it won't be easy. But it's exciting.

Steve Yeah. I bet.

19 ALL TALK

🔲1 **Part 1**

Interviewer On the subject of family secrets, we received an e-mail fom Liz Davison. Liz says that she can't keep secrets from her mother about anything, but that her sister, Kate, is extremely secretive. So Liz, have you got any examples of your extreme honesty?

Liz Well I suppose the, er, most interesting times are when I've been very very honest about Kate.

Interviewer I see. So, what sort of things have you told your mother about Kate, then?

Part 2

Interviewer So, what sort of things have you told your mother about Kate, then?

Liz Oh, there was the occasion when she was at university when she she went to France for the weekend to see her boyfriend and you know, without telling our parents or anything.

Interviewer And you thought that this was, er ...

Liz That's right, I thought they should know. So I, you know, told them where Kate was and what she was doing, and then I asked them not to tell Kate that I had told them.

Part 3

Interviewer So when did you find out, then, Kate, that your parents knew all about it?

Kate Well, it was a little embarrassing really 'cause I, I decided a few months later, when it was all finished,

Interviewer You weren't with the boyfriend any more.

Kate That's right, and I decided that I could probably tell my mother what had happened, and so I told her, but of course, she knew already, and it, it was quite disappointing not to shock her as much as I thought I would.

Interviewer Yes, I can see that. So so, Liz, what ...

🔲2

1 A The police are not investigating because there is no evidence.
   B But I understand that he does have links with the casino business.
   A All I can say for the moment is that these are only rumours – they have no basis in fact.

2 D But I can't believe he said that!
   C No, he told me yesterday morning. He said, 'I've never really loved her.'
   D But that's just ... I mean, he must be really upset to say something like that.

3 E Who do you think the father was then?
   F Well, Anita, I reckon it was Mick Jagger. She was seeing him at about the right time.
   E Yes, I heard that too. I can't remember who told me. But personally, I don't believe it.

4 G So, what's the latest, Jim?
   H Well, apparently this has been his life's dream. He told reporters this morning that he intends to create the greatest art collection in the world.

5 I So, Michael, can we believe the story?
   J Well, nobody knows for sure. Everyone here seems to believe it but no one can agree on the details. Some people say it's the Catholic Church, but I also heard that he's been involved with the Christian Scientists.

20 ALL CHANGE

🔲1 **Part 1**

A So Annette, Simpson Television has bought up more than sixty game shows, including Going for Gold, The Price is Right, What's My Line and, Britain's favourite, Blind Date, and they want to sell them around the world. So, is this another example of globalization? Do you think that one day, everyone in the world will be watching Blind Date? And would we want to?

B Well, I think the answers are no and no. I ...

A Well, that's good news.

B I think that you can divide the world into four cultural continents, and I think Simpson would have the best luck in the western cultural continent, which includes not just the West, but also Australia and New Zealand.

A And why is that?

B Well, the world is still a lot more diverse than most people think. There are a lot of places where people don't have the consumer interest for big prize shows, like The Price is Right. And dating games like Blind Date would not do well in more, er, conservative, religious societies like the Islamic world. But I think quiz shows like Going for Gold would probably be the most successful.

A Because they are thought to be more intelligent, with some educational value?

B Yes.

Part 2

B But I think quiz shows like Going for Gold would probably be the most successful.

A Because they are thought to be more intelligent, with some educational value?

B Yes. And there are other differences, for example, in Japan, and many other countries, they don't like to see ordinary people on television programmes – they like to see celebrities on television. And in a lot of countries, they think that prize winners are getting too much for doing too little. They don't like to see people winning such enormous prizes.

A So you don't think that the game show is finally bringing us to the globalization that everyone talks about?

B Well, no, and I wouldn't want to see it either.

🔲3

Yvonne You said you've always wanted a car. And you could ask Ali to look at it for you, check that it's all right before you buy it.

Anita Yeah, but I couldn't afford that. It's a lot of money.

Yvonne Then how about a bike? That would get you into college on time.

Anita I suppose so. I've never ridden a bike before.

Yvonne You could take lessons. Why don't you?

Anita And what would I do when I go home?

Yvonne You could sell it.

Anita Mmm. Trouble is, we couldn't go to the seaside together on it, could we?

Yvonne Well, I don't know.

Anita Plus it wouldn't be very nice in winter when it's raining and cold.

Yvonne No.

Anita And anyway, I don't really see myself on a bike.

Yvonne No, I suppose not. But it would be good fun turning up on a bike – watch out, here comes Anita the Hell's Angel.

Anita On a two-fifty, yeah.

OXFORD
UNIVERSITY PRESS

Great Clarendon Street, Oxford OX2 6DP

Oxford University Press is a department of the University of Oxford. It furthers the University's objective of excellence in research, scholarship, and education by publishing worldwide in

Oxford New York

Athens Auckland Bangkok Bogotà Buenos Aires Cape Town Chennai Dar es Salaam Delhi Florence Hong Kong Istanbul Karachi Kolkata Kuala Lumpur Madrid Melbourne Mexico City Mumbay Nairobi Paris São Paulo Shanghai Singapore Taipei Tokyo Toronto Warsaw

with associated companies in Berlin Ibadan

Oxford and Oxford English are registered trade marks of Oxford University Press in the UK and in certain other countries

© Oxford University Press 2000

Database right Oxford University Press (maker)

First published 2000
Fourth impression 2001

ISBN 0-19-434078-3

Printed in Italy by Poligrafico Dehoniano

Acknowledgements

The Publisher and Author would like to thank the following for their kind permission to use articles, extracts, or adaptations from copyright material:

Best Magazine for 'There's an axeman in my bedroom!' by Fiona Locke 3 February 1998.
The Guardian for 'A world apart together' by Annie Youngman 13 August 1996; 'Crash made salesman "too nice"' by Luke Harding 21 March 1998; 'Parents' role a model for life' by Martin Kettle 7 November 1996 © The Guardian 1996.
Independent Newspapers (UK) Limited for 'If you want to learn how to speak Russian, get a dog' by Phil Reeves *The Independent* 14 February 1996.
New Internationalist for 'I would pick more daises' by Nadine Stair from February 1995 (issue 264).
Random House UK Limited for 'What am I doing here?' by Bruce Chatwin, published by Jonathan Cape.
Top Santé magazine for 'Testing times?' August 1995 issue.
TV Quick Magazine at H Bauer Publishing: 'Once I was worth 5 camels. Now I can earn £5,000 a day!' by Elaine Pearson from *TV Quick*, 5–11 August 1995 (issue 31).

Every effort has been made to trace and contact copyright holders prior to publication, but in some cases this has not been possible. We apologize for any apparent infringement of copyright, and if notified, the publisher will be pleased to rectify any errors or omissions at the earliest opportunity.

Illustrations by:

James Browne pp.17,18, 44, 57. 59, 69, 70
Ian Kellas pp.36, 39, 45, 49, 53, 66, 74, 78, 82
Julian Mosedale pp.19, 34, 58
Technical graphics pp.11, 14, 99 (maps)

Commissioned Photography by:

Mark Mason p.41 (family)
Maggie Milner pp.20(teenager), 44 (cafe, shop)
Thanks to Brazz in Taunton for permission to photograph on their premises.

The publishers would like to thank the following for their kind permission to reproduce the following photographs:

Associated Press p.9 (Zaherruddin Abdulah); Best Magazine p.46; BBC p.12; Catherine Blackie p.24 (young couple); Bubbles pp.23 (Dr Hercules Robinson), 32 (Frans Rombout /boy on telephone); Chester Beatty Library, Dublin /Bridgeman Art Library p.65; Collections pp.12 (elderly), 32 (camping), 47 (carnival), 62 (girl); Corbis p.56; The Guardian p.24 (Ann Phiri); Robert Harding Picture Library pp.11, 12 (Hanbury Tenison/ children), 16 (Nik Wheeler/bus), 19 (Roy Rainford/ Boston), 26 (Simon Harris/Hong Kong), 28 (Gary Bigham/ parachuting), 30 (Liason/rafting), (48 Jeff Greenberg/ man), 60 (Gavin Hellier/Nepal), 62 (Ron Behrmann/ hot air balloon), 64, 76 (Robert Frerck), 83 (village); Hulton Getty pp.13, 26 (bus stop, children playing); Image Bank pp.16 (diving), 37 (Juan Silva), 63 (woman gesticulating); Impact Photos pp.6 (Andy Johnstone), 7 (Alain Le Garsmeur/ wedding), 12 (Peter Arkell/ teenagers, Ben Gibson/family), 16 (Bruce Stephens/ picnic), 21 (Christophe Bluntzer), 32 (Andy Johnstone/ pub), 35 (John Cole/man on mobile phone), 36 (Mark Henley), 42 (Simon Shepheard), 47 (Ben Edwards/ funeral), 60 (Stephen Sandon/Bangkok), 65 (Keith Cardwell/ Guilin mountains); Leeds Museums and Galleries (City Art Gallery) U.K. Bridgeman Art Library p.22; London Weekend Television p.80 (Blind Date); Magnum pp.7 (Eli Reed/ family), 47 (Fred Mayer/ wedding, Stuart Franklin/Beijing); Kippa Matthews p.24 (Eunice & John Jackson); Network Photographers pp.7 (Alex Segre / cafe); The Oxford Mail p.14 (Miguel Hilario Manina); Pearson Television p. 80 (Sale of the Century, Family Feud); Phoenix Art Museum, Arizona / Bridgeman Art Library p.101; Rex Features pp.28 (shark), 30 (PRC/ dolphins), 32 (Sipa/football), 35 (girl in anorak), 40 (Tim Rooke); Science Photo Library pp.53 (Mehau Kulik/ brain), 72 (Tek Image), 73 (Lynette Cook), 83 (NASA); Tony Stone pp.8 (Marcus Brooke), 17 (Andy Scaks), 28 (Amiuell/ Rugby, Peter Dokus/drinking, Mitch Kezar/fishing, Don Johnston/driving), 29 (Joe McBridge), 30 (Richard Elliott/hiking), 32 (Peter Correz/cycling), 48 (David Young Wolff/ girl), 54 (Dale Durfree), 78 (Karen Moskowitz), 81 (Daniel Bosler/ lady, Tamara Reynolds/man, Frank Siteman/girl); Topham Picturepoint pp.24 (couple jiving), 35 (man on bench and woman on bike with mobile phones), 61; Touchstone Pictures/Kobal Collection p.39

The cartoon on p.54 is © The New Yorker Collection 1958 Richard McCallister from *cartoonbank.com* All Rights Reserved
The cartoon on p. 63 is ©The New Yorker Collection 1955 Ed Fisher from *cartoonbank.com* All Rights Reserved
Grandma Moses: Home of Hezekiah King, 1776, Copyright © 1963 (renewed 1991) on p.101 is reproduced by kind permission of Grandma Moses Properties Co., New York.

Author's acknowledgements

I would like to thank Sue, Guy, Louis, (and Oscar) for putting up with the 'work in progress', and all those who let me record them for the book: Mick and Lyn, and Steve and Gilly of University College, Chichester; the students of Chichester Technical College; neighbours Andy, Vicky, Becky, and Tom; and Lindsey and Diana. Many thanks.